Stepping Out

A Comedy

Richard Harris

Samuel French - London
New York - Toronto - Hollywood

STEPPING OUT

First presented at the Thorndike Theatre, Leatherhead.
Subsequently presented by Bill Kenwright, in association
with the Thorndike Theatre, at the Duke of York's
Theatre, London on 18th September, 1984, with the
following cast:

Mavis	Barbara Ferris
Mrs Fraser	Sheri Shepstone
Lynne	Charlotte Barker
Dorothy	Josephine Gordon
Maxine	Barbara Young
Andy	Gabrielle Lloyd
Geoffrey	Ben Aris
Sylvia	Diane Langton
Rose	Peggy Phango
Vera	Marcia Warren

The part of the unseen Stage Manager was played by
David Emerson. Other parts were played by Ann
Gabrielle, Sue Scott-Davison and Eileen Dunwoodie.
These parts (two "extras" at the beginning of the play
and the two sugar-plum fairies in Act II) may be omitted
if desired*

Directed by Julia McKenzie
Designed by Stuart Stanley
Finale choreography by Tudor Davies
Choreography within the play by Jenifer Mary Morgan

The action takes place in a North London church hall

Time—the present

*See note on p. v

NOTE ON CASTING
The dialogue and stage directions in square brackets on pages 2, 3 and 70 are to be omitted if the two extra characters at the beginning of the play, and the two sugar plum fairies, are not included in the cast

The asterisked line of Mavis's dialogue on page 3 will also need to be altered to read: "Did Maxine pay for last week?"

The role of Rose must be played by an Afro-Caribbean actress and not by a white woman blacked-up or by, or as, any other nationality. However, if it is not possible to cast an Afro-Caribbean, then the role may be played by an Asian as an Asian.

See page 78 for extensive Dance Notes

ACT I

SCENE 1

A church hall in North London. Just before eight o'clock, a February evening

The hall is wooden-walled with an open girder roof. Most of the rear wall is taken up by a raised stage with steps leading up to it. Rear of the stage is a semi-glazed door leading through to the changing room. R of the stage, and set at an angle, a pair of semi-glazed swing doors lead through to the unseen entrance lobby. Upstage in the L wall are a pair of doors which are marked as the fire exit. These doors have a crash bar—used by some of the dancers as a practice barre. High up in each of the side walls is an uncurtained and dusty window. There are pull chords, but the windows are obviously never opened. Metal stacking chairs are arranged along both side walls and along the front of the stage. There are three elderly gasfires, not turned on at the moment. An ancient fire extinguisher displayed on each of the side walls. On the stage, there is a small untidy pile of chairs next to the changing room door, and a notice-board on legs. Pinned on the board are various notices and posters—showing the activities that go on in the hall—dancing, scouts, WRVS etc. DL is a low upright piano and stool. Next to these, a folding table which holds the class register and a small metal cashbox. The "fourth wall" is the unseen practice mirror

At rise of CURTAIN

Mavis—the teacher—sits on a downstage chair, near the piano, smoking a cigarette and using a tin lid as an ashtray. She is an ex-pro dancer, attractive, 40. She wears a T-shirt, bright see-through tights, long legwarmers and ballet shoes. A man's sweater is knotted around her shoulders—she's keeping warm after taking a ballet class. She takes up a small carton of fruit juice and sips it through a straw as she looks at, without really watching . . .

Dorothy is practising a ballet step using the back of a chair, downstage c watching herself intently in the mirror and being encouraged by Lynne. Dorothy is small, anxious and birdlike, could be anything from 30 to 45 and is somewhere in between. She wears a black leotard, ballet shoes and has an elasticated bandage round one knee. There is a hint of white knicker showing beneath the leotard. Lynne is 19. She is eager to please, has a lovely face but is of large proportions. She never wears make-up and her skin glows healthily. She wears a tracksuit top, black tights, rumpled legwarmers and scuffed ballet shoes

Mrs Fraser, the pianist, sits at the piano reading a woman's magazine and finishing off an apple. She is fiftyish, a square-shaped Northern lady who prides herself on her pessimism. She wears a tweed overcoat, knitted hat and clumpy brogues and can more often than not be seen chewing some form of fruit. [A Young Woman in crash helmet, bright tracksuit, legwarmers and running shoes, stands making a note of something on the notice board]

Maxine and Andy stand near the chairs, R. Their topcoats and bags are on two of the chairs. Maxine is delving into her copious holdall which contains leotards etc. in their plastic packs. She is in the process of doing a selling job on Andy. Andy is tall and thin and in her mid-30s. She wears a long cardigan over a floral dress, beige thick stockings and court shoes. She has short hair and wears large glasses. She is rather inclined to stoop as though ashamed of her height. Maxine is a good-looking forty-something. She has dyed blond hair and good make-up. She wears a tight red leotard over a black jumper, tight black shiny trousers and long red legwarmers. There are big rocks on her fingers

Lynne There you are, you see, you've got it.
Dorothy Was it better?
Lynne It was really good — look, look in the mirror — your back's ever so straight and everything.
Dorothy And everything — yes. (*Dorothy has the habit of joining in on the last two or three words of whatever is said to her. Sometimes she even gets there first*) It did feel better.
Lynne It was really good, wasn't it, Mavis?
Mavis (*who wasn't really watching*) You're doing very well, Dorothy — off you go now ladies and get your taps on.

She smiles, stubbing out her cigarette. Mrs Fraser makes great play of waving away smoke that is anyway nowhere near her. Dorothy moves the chair back against the wall and takes up her handbag — where she goes, the handbag goes too — and she and Lynne move obediently to the changing room, with

Dorothy Only I worry you see.
Lynne You mustn't worry about it.
Dorothy About it — no — I mean, it's only for fun, isn't it?
Lynne Of course it is.
Dorothy Is — yes.
Mavis (*calling after them*) You're doing very well, Dorothy.
Mrs Fraser (*to herself, but loud and clear*) Oh yes? (*She licks a thumb and turns the magazine page*)

Dorothy and Lynne go into the changing room

Mavis takes a pair of tap shoes from her canvas bag and changes them for the ballet shoes as

Maxine What are you— a thirty-six?
Andy Umm ... thirty-four — well, thirty-three actually.

Maxine takes a blue and white striped leotard from its pack and holds it up against Andy, guiding her so that they are looking into the mirror as

Maxine (*admiringly*) Oh yes.

Andy You don't think, um, sleeves, do you?

Maxine Not in the blue, no, can't help you. I could do you sleeves in the red, but with your colouring, I don't think so.

Andy Might you be getting some in?

Maxine I can never tell—I get what's on offer, you know what I mean?

Mrs Fraser (*not looking up*) I know what you mean.

Andy Umm ... might I just have a look at the red?

Maxine Have a look at what you like, darling. (*And she sorts out a red leotard*)

[*A Middle-aged Woman, swathed in headscarf and anorak and carrying a bulging Waitrose bag and one of Maxine's leotards, comes quickly out of the changing room. She and the Young Woman exit quickly, as though late, with*

Woman ThankseversomuchMavis, seeyounextweekthen 'night.

The others—apart from Mrs Fraser—chorus their good-nights

The two women go out]

Mavis Did she pay for last week?*

Mrs Fraser She did when I reminded her. (*She doesn't look up from her magazine. She seldom looks directly at anyone*)

Maxine is holding a long-sleeved red and white leotard against Andy. They look into the mirror as

Maxine No, I don't think so ... it's the blue, definitely the blue. (*And she holds up the blue one, swivelling Andy towards Mavis, with*) Wouldn't you say, Mavis, the blue?

Mavis It's very nice, yes, I like it.

Maxine There y'go then, Andy, three quid.

Andy Yes, well, all right, fine.

And the transaction will be completed as

Geoffrey enters. He is tall, in his mid-40s. The sort of man who doesn't like being noticed and most of the time wouldn't be. He wears a raincoat over a rather worn suit, carries a briefcase

Maxine Hello Geoffrey, how's Geoffrey?

He manages a smile and hovers with

Geoffrey Umm ... someone's left their lights on, I think it's you, er, Mavis—the Volkswagen.

Mavis Oh Christ not again, thanks, Geoffrey.

Mrs Fraser (*reading*) You'll ruin that car.

Geoffrey If you'd like to give me the key, I'll um ...

Mavis Would you mind, thanks—(*she tosses him the keys*)—you're a love.

He makes to go out again but Maxine holds up the red leotard with

Maxine How about a nice leotard, Geoffrey—if you don't fancy wearing it
now, you can wear it on the beach.

Geoffrey goes out

Maxine nudges Andy and squeezes the crotch of the leotard

Plenty of room for his wallet.

*Maxine and Andy sit to put on their tap shoes. Maxine's are old and soft,
Andy's shiny new*

Mavis Bloody car.

Mrs Fraser You'll forget your head one of these days.

Mavis Yes, all right Glenda, thank you.

Mrs Fraser No wonder people take advantage.

Maxine (*to Andy*) How are you off for tights?

Mrs Fraser If it was me, I'd say something.

Mavis I said thank you, Glenda.

Mrs Fraser Turning the place into a bazaar. (*She does her thumb-licking
page-turning routine*)

*Vera enters. She hasn't been here before but is undaunted. She is 35, neat
and proper as a pin, wears an expensive belted fawn raincoat and high heels,
carries a good leather bag. Her dyed red hair and make-up are immaculate.
But for all her primness, she dresses in a way that suggests the high-class
tart*

Vera Excuse me, is this the tap class?

Maxine It certainly is—shop!

Mavis (*moving towards Vera, smiling*) Hello, I'm Mavis, I run the class, can
I help you?

Vera Am I too late to join?

Mavis No, of course you're not.

*Mrs Fraser glances up to give Vera the once-over, then pointedly holds up the
register, already back to reading her magazine. Vera takes the opportunity to
look at herself in the mirror, touching her hair*

This is Mrs Fraser—she's our pianist.

Vera Oh yes—hello.

Mavis Have you done any tap before?

Vera Well I did start another class but—well to be quite honest, I didn't
really like the teacher. (*It's a careful, precise, rather flat accent. The
improved Midlands accent that almost turns "my" into "may"*)

Mavis (*smiling*) I'd better not ask who it was then ... (*she makes to write in
the book*) ... Mrs ...?

Vera Andrews, Mrs Andrews.

Mavis And what do we call you?

Vera Oh—yes—Vera actually.

During this, Geoffrey enters and moves to Mavis with her keys

Mavis Welcome to the class then Vera ... excuse me ... thanks Geoffrey.

Geoffrey moves away to change, where he always changes, behind the notice-board on the stage. Unseen, he puts on a roll-necked sweater, old and baggy dark blue tracksuit trousers, elasticated at the ankles, and a pair of brown boots to which taps have been fitted. He takes his time about changing, so as not to have to make conversation. As

Vera (*looking around*) Are there many?
Mavis (*putting the keys into her bag*) Sorry?
Vera I was wondering how many there were in a class.
Mavis Not too many: just about the right number.
Mrs Fraser Like flies. They come out in the summer and drop off in the winter. Like flies.
Mavis Most of the class are fairly new—apart from Maxine and Lynne who've been with me from the beginning—so you'll have nothing to worry about.
Vera Oh I'm not worried, I pick things up quite quick actually.
Mavis Good.
Vera When would you like me to pay?

Still reading, Mrs Fraser holds out the cashbox

Mrs Fraser Now.
Mavis I usually ask people to pay weekly before each session. (*She smiles*) If you don't come you don't pay.
Vera Oh I shall come—I like to do things properly, there's no point else, is there?

Sylvia comes out of the changing room. She is in her early 30s, a short, bubbly brunette. Her bright and outrageous clothing accentuates her over-ample curves. She wears tatty white plimsolls and chews gum most of the time

Mavis Give them a shout, will you Sylvia?

Sylvia leans back into the door to shout

Sylvia Oi—we're starting! (*And she jumps down from the stage, reacting to the impact and telling herself that she must stop doing that ... and moves to regard herself in the mirror*)

Lynne comes of the changing room. She wears tap shoes and a cardigan over her tights—it matches the legwarmers she has changed into

Lynne Just coming, Mavis—Rose has broken one of her laces.
Mrs Fraser Makes a change.
Sylvia (*of herself, in the mirror*) Talk about the fairy on the bleeding Christmas tree.
Maxine You've lost weight, Sylv.
Sylvia Definitely not.
Maxine Oh you have, hasn't she?
Andy Oh ... at least ...

Vera (*pointing*) Is that where we change?'
Mavis Lynne—will you show ...
Vera No that's all right thank you I can manage. (*She is about to move away but takes up the carton and apple core on top of the piano*)
I'll just get rid of these for you, shall I?
Mavis Oh ... that's very nice of you, Vera, thank you.

Vera carries the debris towards the changing room as Mrs Fraser glances at Mavis ... hello, we've got one of those ...

Vera almost bumps into Dorothy as she hurries out of the changing room. Dorothy now wears a white M & S cardigan over her leotard, and new white tap shoes which have large red laces. Her handbag is over her arm

Dorothy Rose says has anyone got a spare lace she can borrow?
Mavis (*generally*) Rose says has anyone got a spare lace she can borrow.
Dorothy Borrow—yes.
Geoffrey I say—she can, umm ... (*From behind the notice-board, he holds up one of his shoes*)
Mavis Problem over, thank you Geoffrey.

Geoffrey takes the black lace from his shoe and gives it to Dorothy

Dorothy hurries back into the changing room

Sylvia—who has remained looking at herself glumly in the mirror—speaks

Sylvia I ate like a pig this weekend. Saturday it was his firm's dinner dance and Sunday his mother came over so I had to put on a roast, didn't I?
Maxine You were doing so well—wasn't she, she was doing really well.
Sylvia Sod'em that's what I say.

Dorothy hurries out of the changing room and puts her bag under a chair as Mrs Fraser strikes a loud chord on the piano and Mavis claps her hands

Mavis Right—we'll make a start then, shall we?

Maxine and Lynne move directly to the front, but the others are less anxious to exhibit their wares

Let's have you in the front then, shall we Geoffrey? (*She looks pointedly at Mrs Fraser who is still reading*) When you're ready Glenda.

Mrs Fraser unhurriedly sets down the magazine and sorts out the first piece of music

Right—we'll start with some relaxing ... four bends, four swings ... are you with us, Glenda?
Mrs Fraser I'm just getting my bits out, thank you.

Vera comes out of the changing room. She wears a neat skirt and new tap shoes. There is a hankie up her sleeve

Vera So sorry to keep you everyone.
Mavis This is Vera—say hello to Vera everyone.

They chorus their hellos as Vera moves confidently into the front row, admiring herself in the mirror

If you'd like to stay at the back, Vera, then you can see what we're doing.

Vera moves into the back row, unoffended, with a last look and touch of her hair in the mirror, as

Don't worry if you get it wrong, you won't get thrown out, it's not an audition—come forward a bit, Geoffrey—all right, Glenda?

Mrs Fraser When you're ready.

Mavis OK. So it's five six seven eight . . .

And the simple warm-up routine begins (See Dance Notes p. 78). Mavis faces out front, her back to the class—most of whom intently follow her every move, staring at her feet. Mrs Fraser plays ("The Entertainer") in very strict tempo. She never looks at the dancers and whenever she is not actually playing, she goes straight back to her magazine

And we see our class in action for the first time. Lynne is good, light on her feet and attentive. She smiles a lot but bites a nail when she does something wrong. She's very serious about dancing. Dorothy makes extravagantly large movements, is unsmiling and looking all the time at Mavis' feet. Maxine is confident, competent, and enjoying it. She's the best mover in the group, the most "natural" dancer and, unlike most of them, uses her arms well. Andy is hopeless, with no co-ordination whatsoever. She looks doggedly to the front as though trying to suggest that she really isn't here, keeps her arms tight to her sides and her fists clenched. She raises her feet as though avoiding dog's muck. Geoffrey is limited but competent. When he smiles—for instance at a comment on someone else's mistake—it's as though he has forgotten himself and is quick to control it. Sylvia chews gum, isn't very good but doesn't give a damn. She's always that little bit out of step: if the others do something to the left, she's guaranteed to do it to the right. Vera picks it up quickly. She dances as primly and as efficiently as she does everything else

As they dance, Mavis calls out the steps as they come up, dancing along with them . . . smiling a lot over her shoulder on a one-to-one basis and seems to be enjoying it. After all, they come here to have a good time and she's a pro whose job is to make the punters happy. So that they are tapping away and Mavis is calling out the steps as

Rose hurries out of the changing room. She is in her 40s, a large black Trinidadian, wearing an obvious wig, a bright pink dress over black tights and white tap shoes, one of which is done up with Geoffrey's black lace and is already coming undone. She has a large crucifix round her neck and lots of rings on her fingers

(*As they dance*) Evening Rose, nice of you to join us.

Rose hurries to join them as they are moving backwards so that she bumps into Andy before taking her place in the back row. Rose has little sense of rhythm but loves every minute of it. When she makes a mistake, she smiles broadly, covering her mouth with a hand. And they continue dancing as

OK let's try four tap springs and tap step ball change followed by a cramp roll starting with your left foot ... (*and they change the step as*) ... no, Sylvia, your left foot ... no, your other left foot.

Sylvia I can't think and move at the same time, it's not natural.

Mavis Well have a go anyway.

They continue dancing and come to the end of the routine and the music stops and Rose rubs one of her calf muscles and Mavis goes to her

Oh Rose ... has your leg gone numb again?

Rose I don't know, I can't feel it.

Mavis Vera—try and keep the weight on the balls of your feet ... no, your heels on the floor but the weight on your toes, yes?

Vera tries it, looking at herself in the mirror

Something like that, yes ... (*Generally*) You're all still inclined to be a bit heavy—try and keep it light, nice and light—and Sylvia—try and keep your knees together, yes?

Sylvia I've been trying to keep my knees together all my life.

Maxine Haven't we all, darling?

Mavis OK—move forward everyone and let's have the back row in front this time ... (*She indicates for Mrs Fraser to resume playing, but*)

Dorothy You know that bit where you go ... (*she demonstrates*) ... is it toe toe heel heel?

Mavis (*demonstrating*) Toe toe heel heel, yes.

Dorothy I thought so: only I've been going toe heel toe heel.

Andy (*anxiously*) Isn't that what it's supposed to be?

Lynne No, it's like this ... (*And she demonstrates*)

Mavis Have you got it now?

Dorothy Yes thank you—sorry.

Andy Sorry.

Mavis All right Sylvia?

Sylvia has been flapping her feet along with the others

Sylvia I think so, yeah.

Mavis Incidentally, will you be getting some proper tap shoes or what?

Sylvia Now I've mastered it, I suppose I'd better.

Vera (*putting a hand up*) Excuse me.

They regard her

I got mine in Northfields Lane actually—they've got ever such a good selection.

Rose (*who has sat down for a rest*) I wouldn't go into that woman's shop, never again. Not for nothing. That is what I call an awful person.

Vera I thought she was rather helpful actually.

Dorothy Speak as you find, I always say.

Rose Well I'm saying: she's an awful person.

Mavis Right, let's get on, shall we? We'll have a look at the step we learned last week ... you remember ... it's ... (*She starts to demonstrate, but*)

Sylvia Excuse me.
Mavis Yes Sylvia.
Sylvia I wasn't here last week.
Andy (*anxiously*) Neither was I—sorry.
Mavis OK—who was here last week?

Hands go up like children in class

OK, let's have you lot at the front then and the others at the back. There's nothing complicated, we'll go through it very slowly ... basically it's ... (*See Dance Notes p. 78*) (*and she demonstrates as*) ... three buffaloes to the right and a cramp roll ... three buffaloes to the left, cramp roll, four scoops, six tap springs in a circle, tap step stamp stamp ... OK—we'll go through it nice and slowly to the music ... nice and slowly please Glenda ... and it's five six seven eight ...

Mrs Fraser plays—"Tea For Two"—but much too quickly and the dancers stumble and Mavis waves for her to stop, with

No, that's too fast ... take it at ... (*She demonstrates the tempo*)
Mrs Fraser It's exactly the same as last week.
Mavis (*not prepared to argue*) OK—just a little slower then ... and it's five six seven eight ...

Mrs Fraser plays again at exactly the same tempo

Glenda, it's still too fast.
Mrs Fraser It's exactly the same as last week.
Maxine No, it was slower last week—I mean, it doesn't affect me, but ...
Rose Yes, it was definitely slower, definitely.
Dorothy Definitely—yes, wasn't it, Geoffrey—wouldn't you say?
Geoffrey Umm ...
Mavis OK, here we go then ... five six seven eight ...

Mrs Fraser plays at funereal pace and the dancers stumble

Glenda ... it's too slow.
Mrs Fraser You said it was too fast.
Mavis And now I'm saying it's too slow.

A moment

Mrs Fraser I see. (*She closes the piano lid and stands*) When you've made up your mind, no doubt you'll let me know.

Without looking at anyone, she goes into the changing room

All the others, apart from Vera, are used to this performance

Mavis Excuse me ... (*She moves to the changing room with*) Take them through it again, will you Lynne?

She exits into the changing room

There is a moment's silence

Vera Does she often get upset?

Sylvia I think she's going through the change of key myself.

Lynne Which bit did she mean?

Dorothy I think she meant the last bit.

Rose has moved to sit, adjusting her wig

Geoffrey Excuse me, um, Rose—my lace is undone.

Lynne (*to Dorothy*) Was it hop hop step turn . . .?

Dorothy Like this.

She slowly demonstrates with her large movements and Lynne joins in as

Vera I did consider aerobics.

Sylvia Oh I've done all that so I thought, right, now I've cracked the body beautiful, I'll move it about a bit.

Vera There are so many classes nowadays, aren't there? Everyone I know seems to be going to some class or another.

Rose That's because we're a very class-conscious society.

Maxine (*to Vera*) That's a nice shirt: you didn't get it locally, I bet.

Vera No, Lionel brought it back from Geneva.

Sylvia You coming for a drink after, Rose?

Rose Are you going?

Sylvia Course I'm going, come on, come for a drink.

Maxine is doing some steps in front of the mirror

Vera You're ever so good at it, have you been doing it long?

Maxine Don't tell anyone but I used to be an Ovaltinie.

Dorothy is practising a ballet step, looking intently into the mirror

Vera I thought about ballet, but . . .

Mavis comes out of the changing room, followed by Mrs Fraser who is adjusting her hat. Mavis moves straight to the front of the class and Mrs Fraser returns to her piano—as though nothing has happened

Mavis (*clapping her hands*) OK sorry about that, slight misunderstanding, my fault, let's do it again—are we ready? And it's five six seven eight . . .

Mrs Fraser resumes playing "Tea For Two"—and this time at the right tempo—to Mavis' obvious relief—and they dance, with Mavis calling out the steps and they continue

And a little faster please, Glenda . . .

They continue, the music a little faster now . . . with Sylvia colliding into Vera who says sorry . . . and they go through the routine with Mavis leading from the front and they finish, banging their feet more or less together on the last step and they hold their pose for a brief moment and——

The Lights go quickly to Black-out. At the same time, the orchestrated version of "Happy Feet" comes up—underscored with heavy tap dancing. The music continues then suddenly stops as the Lights come up for the next scene

SCENE 2

*The same. A month later, 7. 45 p.m. It is cold outside and those arriving show
signs of it*

*Geoffrey sits in front of the stage, trying to remove the clingfilm wrapping from
a sandwich. He has his raincoat draped around his shoulders and has already
changed into his dance gear*

*After a moment, Vera bustles in. She is wearing a leather overcoat trimmed
in fur, and long polished boots. She carries her holdall and a Harrods bag*

*They are somewhat surprised at seeing each other. He is rather awkward at
being caught with his sandwich*

Vera Oh hello Geoffrey, you're early.
Geoffrey Yes, I—came straight from the office.
Vera It's all rush nowadays, isn't it?
Geoffrey (*standing*) Usually I have time to go home, but, ummm . . . (*he
vaguely indicates his sandwich*)
Vera Oh don't mind me—would you like some coffee, I brought some
coffee—yes of course you would . . .

*She gives him the metal cup from the flask and pours coffee into it. The cup
gets very hot and he can just about hold it between his fingers—not that Vera
notices, as:*

I get really thirsty when I'm dancing, don't you? I think all the girls do.
I'm surprised they haven't got a kettle here or something, there is a plug. I
might suggest it actually. You don't work locally then, Geoffrey?
Geoffrey No, no, in the city.
Vera Oh yes? What sort of work is that—you don't mind my asking, do
you?
Geoffrey Insurance—shipping insurance.
Vera That must be very interesting.

Before he can protest, she is spooning unwanted sugar into his coffee with:

Sugar? (*She returns the flask to her bag as:*) Anyway, if you'll excuse me, I
just want to have a go at the toilet. (*She produces a lavatory brush from her
bag*) That's why I came early. Not being funny or anything, but it's not
very nice in there, is it?
Geoffrey I don't think I've ever actually, umm. . .
Vera I mean, all manner of people use it during the week, don't they, it's not
just us, is it? You have to be so careful. Don't hurry your coffee, I can
wash the cup out later.

*She goes into the changing room. Geoffrey quickly finishes the coffee,
holding the cup out to her, but she is already gone. He is moving to put the
clingfilm into the bin by the piano when Andy enters. She wears a duffle coat
over her dance outfit, carries a bag. She smiles, a little shy at finding him on
his own, and pushes back the hood of her duffle coat*

Andy Hello.
Geoffrey (*returning her smile*) Vera's here. (*He makes a small gesture towards the changing room*) She's—um—doing the ablutions.
Andy Oh dear.

A slight moment

Geoffrey She's rather ...
Andy Yes.

Again, that little smile from each of them. We should sense that they very much want to communicate. A moment

Mavis is late.
Geoffrey Yes, she's usually here by now.
Andy No Mrs Fraser either.
Geoffrey No. I think Mavis usually gives her a lift.
Andy Yes.

She gives a slight shiver. Geoffrey takes out a lighter and will light the three fires, so that his back is turned to her as

Do you live in Hartington Road?
Geoffrey Ellesmere—it's just off Hartington.
Andy I ask because I saw you walking up there the other evening—Tuesday I think it was.
Geoffrey I go round that way from the station—up Hartington and round the crescent—it's just that little bit quicker than ...

He makes a little gesture indicating "round the other way". She nods

Do you live that ...?
Andy No, no, we're in Parkside.

Geoffrey nods appreciatively

I was going that way to collect one of my old ladies—I help out at the blind club every month—just fetching and carrying really—it's not much but at least it gets them out of the house—some of the older ones are completely alone, you know—it seems so awful, they never speak to a living soul from ... (*She realizes she's going on a bit and—with a smile as though making light of it*) I almost offered you a lift. Perhaps next time.
Geoffrey Yes, that would be——

Vera comes out of the changing room

Vera Geoffrey, can you give me a ... oh hello Andy you look nice, sorry— can you give me a hand, I can't get the thing in.
Geoffrey Yes of course. (*He pulls off his raincoat. He is wearing a handknit-ted multi-coloured pullover over a shirt. So that he is already on his way into the changing room as*)
Vera (*to Andy*) Sorry to interrupt.
Andy You weren't interrup——
Vera Thankseversomuch Geoffrey.

Geoffrey goes into the changing room

Vera almost goes after him but instead takes up the cup, indicating it to Andy with

Vera Best do it now before I forget, eh? (*And she almost goes back inside; confidentially*) He's very brave, isn't he, Andy? Being the only one with all us girls. I mean, he must feel very awkward at times, mustn't he?

Andy I've never really . . .

Vera I wonder why he comes?

Andy Perhaps you should ask him.

Vera I did—he says he enjoys it.

Andy Well then.

Vera Yes, I suppose so. (*Even more confidentially*) His wife's dead, you know. (*She mouths, rather than says, the word*) Cancer. Forty-two.

Andy And his son is in Canada, yes I know.

Vera Vancouver. He's an architect. I expect that's it then, he enjoys the company. Oh yes, I hope you don't mind but I've been meaning to ask you—what is Andy short for?

Andy It's not short for anything—it's long for Ann.

• **Vera** Oh.

She goes into the changing room

Andy makes to take the scarf from round her neck, but changes her mind and sits to take out her tap shoes as

Sylvia and Rose enter. Sylvia wears a short coney coat over her dance gear. Rose wears a neat M & S raincoat and headscarf. Each carries a bag with shoes etc in. As they enter

Rose Half-past nine he finally rolls in. "Where've you been," I say . . . "We'll discuss that later," he say . . . "in the meantime, dearly beloved, where's my dinner?"

Sylvia (*chewing gum*) Watcha do—throw it at him?

Rose It was already in the bin—so I threw the bin at him. (*She's already on her way into the changing room, giggling as*) Holy Jesus and Mary, the look on that man's face! (*And then, like a roll of thunder*) Next time I'll kill him!

She goes into the changing room

Sylvia moves to regard herself unlovingly in the mirror

Sylvia No, don't you believe a word of it, she's dotty about him. They're dotty about each other. He's quite a good looker for a man of his age.

Andy Is he . . . um . . .?

Sylvia What—black? Yeah, blacker than she is. But phenomenal bone structure and beautiful nails, I noticed. Not like my Terry's . . . hands like the soles of your feet. He was a scaffolder. He'd have to be, wouldn't he, to get up this lot. (*A moment as she regards herself in the mirror*) We met 'em for a drink one evening . . . holding hands they were, looking into each other's eyes, whispering sweet do-da's ... he even holds the door open for her.

Andy That must be—very nice.

Sylvia (*moving to warm her behind by a fire*) Twenty years married and three kids, more like a rotten miracle. Mind you, they're very religious, I wonder if that's got anything to do with it?

Andy I don't know. I don't think so. I'd like to think so but ...

Sylvia Are you religious then?

Andy No. No, not at all.

Sylvia I'm a Catholic you know. Vaguely. My father's Irish—he did a bit when he was younger but his heart wasn't in it, you know what I mean? No, luck of the draw, innit? Sometimes I look at my Terry and I think what are you doing with this person but then again I think to myself, Sylv, bearing in mind the gaping holes in your own personality, you are a very lucky girl. I must have a pee, I'm bursting.

Maxine enters. She is wearing a full-length suede coat and silk scarf over her dance gear, carries her tap shoes and a bag with two new shirts in it

Maxine Evening Andy how's Andy hello Sylvia how's Sylvia?

Sylvia (*over her shoulder, going into the changing room*) Hello Maxine—had a good week, have you?

She gives a big wink to Andy and goes into the changing room

Maxine slumps into a chair, stretching out her legs and reaching for her cigarettes and lighter

Maxine What a day, I'm lucky to be alive. Don't ask me what happened, I might tell you. (*She attempts to use her lighter which doesn't work*) The whole day I'm on red alert. I really didn't think I was going to make it tonight, every time I open the door the phone rings—is it for me? Forget it, I'm just the answering service, it's for Wonderboy. I should have his social life, what do they see in him? You wouldn't have a light by any chance?

Andy Sorry.

Maxine Anyway. I'm here please God and that's all I care about.

Andy (*smiling*) You really enjoy these classes, don't you?

Maxine Hooked, darling, hooked. So how are you?

Andy Fine.

Maxine You want me to be honest? You don't look fine. You look like you could do with a break.

Andy (*trying to make it sound light*) Why do you say things like that?

Geoffrey comes out of the changing room

Maxine Hello Geoffrey how's Geoffrey? Before I forget—I brought you those shirts—(*she tosses the bag to him as he moves to her*)—if you don't like them, bring them back next week, OK?

Geoffrey How much do I ...?

Maxine Don't worry about it, we'll sort it out next week.

Dorothy enters. She wears moonboots, trousers, an anorak with yellow safety harness, carries a bicycle basket containing her handbag, lamp, pump and dancegear

Dorothy Evening everyone.

She goes straight through into the changing room

Maxine takes off her coat and puts on her tap shoes as Geoffrey takes the package and puts it into his briefcase as

Maxine (*to Andy*) I know, I'm terrible, I should mind my own business. But do yourself a favour, get him to take you away for a couple of days, it works wonders, believe me.

Andy stands, taking up her bag

Andy (*stiffly, aware of Geoffrey*) Yes, well, I'm afraid that isn't possible at the moment.

Andy goes into the changing room

Maxine sees Geoffrey looking at her

Maxine If you want something it's possible, believe me it's possible.

Sylvia comes out of the changing room

Sylvia She's only at it again.
Maxine Who is?
Sylvia Wassername—Vera. (*She sits on the floor, taking out a pair of new tap shoes*)
Maxine What is it this time?
Sylvia She's only sticking up a list of instructions about the toilet facilities.
Maxine Like your shoes, Sylv.

Rose, now in her dancing gear, comes out of the changing room, giggling to herself

Sylvia What are you so cheerful about?
Rose Nothing, nothing.
Maxine Vera's just given her nine out of ten for toilet training.

Rose sits and, still smiling to herself

Rose Do you ever make love first thing in the morning?
Sylvia Are you kidding? He can't do a thing until he's had a cooked breakfast.
Maxine Your boy got himself a job yet, Rose?
Rose Everywhere he try, it's the same story.
Sylvia I think it's bleeding lousy for kids nowadays.
Rose All the time he was at school, we keep telling him—no qualifications, no work.
Sylvia If you ask me all this qualifications lark is just an excuse—(*tapping her head*)—it's what you got up here—right, Geoffrey?

Rose (*insisting*) He should have paid more attention at school.
Maxine Do any of 'em?
Rose For some, it's more important than others.
Sylvia He'll sort himself out, don't worry.
Geoffrey What about the Youth Training Scheme?
Rose He say it's slave labour.
Sylvia He's right an'all.
Geoffrey Well I would have thought it at least . . .
Rose And the way he talk to his father. We never bring up our children to talk like that.
Maxine They're all the same. Look at Wonderboy: one minute he's in a pop group and the next minute he's in a coma. D'you know what the latest is? He's decided he wants to go to art school. Art school? He can't even draw a deep breath without fainting.

Andy comes out of the changing room with her bag. She wears the new leotard, still has the scarf around her neck, is rather self-conscious

The others see her in the mirror

Maxine ⎫   ⎧ Nice, very very nice.
Sylvia ⎬ (*together*) ⎨ Pretty, Andy.
Rose ⎭   ⎩ Yes.

Dorothy comes out of the changing room, with her bag

Dorothy Does anyone know what's happening?
Andy Yes, it's nearly eight o'clock—do you think Mavis is coming or what?
Maxine Yes, where is she?
Sylvia She must be coming.
Andy Something could have happened.
Sylvia (*of her body*) Don't tell me I've brought this lot here for nothing.
Rose Don't worry, ladies—if the worst comes to the worst, I'll take the class. (*And she demonstrates her dancing ability*)
Sylvia I thought you lot could move.
Rose Sure we can move. The problem being in my case that it all move in different directions.
Sylvia Careful, you'll knock your wig off.
Maxine Is it growing out yet, Rose?
Rose My old man say it's like sleeping with a Brillo pad.
Sylvia Another three months and it'll be all lovely and curly again.
Rose But that's the whole point: I wanted it lovely and straight.
Maxine You should always read the instructions on the bottle.
Sylvia Failing which, you should always try it out on the dog.
Maxine If it says "professional use only", it means——
Rose Jesus Christ don't preach! I got enough trouble. (*She does a few more steps*) Look at me—if the bloody wig isn't falling off I'm knocking myself senseless with the crucifix.
Andy Is Lynne here—she can start the class surely—she knows all the steps.
Dorothy Lynne isn't coming this week.

Rose That's right, she's working.
Dorothy Working—yes.
Andy Anyway, we can't start, we haven't got any music.
Maxine Yes, where's Mrs Fraser?
Sylvia She'll be round the boozer, selling her body. (*She takes gum from her mouth and replaces it with a new piece*)
Geoffrey I imagine she's with Mavis.
Maxine Can anyone play the piano?
Sylvia Well she can't for a start.
Rose Who needs the piano. (*Cod-West Indian*) Just follow me, girls, I got music in ma soul.

Vera comes out of the changing room. She wears leotard, legwarmers. She carries two ashtrays and a wastebin. She moves straight to Sylvia with

Vera Excuse me . . . I hope you don't mind my asking but do you chew gum because you've given up smoking?
Sylvia No—because I might meet someone nice.
Vera Only I keep finding it everywhere.
Sylvia That's because I keep putting it everywhere. (*She drops the gum noisily into the bin*) I couldn't half do with someone like you at home, Vera.

Vera puts the bin down and distributes the ashtrays as Maxine moves to Rose

Maxine The reason I ask about your boy, Rose . . . I've got a job coming up at the end of the month. The money's not much but the opportunities there if he keeps his nose clean. Anyway, if he's interested, you know where the shop is, ask him to come and see me.

A moment

Rose Thank you, Maxine. I'll tell him.
Andy Well I think we should do something, don't you?
Vera Have we got a problem?
Dorothy Mavis isn't here.
Vera Do you think she might not be coming then?
Dorothy She might have had an emergency.
Vera We could always give her a ring.
Maxine Has anyone got the number?
Vera Yes I have as a matter of fact.
Maxine Who'd have guessed?
Vera I always take people's numbers—well, you never know, do you?
Sylvia You haven't taken mine.
Vera You know what I mean.
Sylvia No I don't.
Geoffrey Might I make a suggestion?
Rose Geoffrey is about to make a suggestion.
Maxine Here, Geoffrey, I hope your sex life is as busy as that pullover.

Andy moves to one side, irritation growing, as

Rose Now then ladies, let the man speak.
Sylvia Order!
Vera Yes, come on Geoffrey, what were you going to say?
Geoffrey All I was going to say was ... why don't we start the warm-up
while we're waiting. That was all, really.
Sylvia That is brilliant. Brilliant.
Rose All those in favour of starting the warm-up?

Various hands go up

Rose All those against?
Andy (*a sudden flash of irritation*) Oh come on this is ridiculous.

They all turn to regard her, surprised

I'm sorry, it's just ... it's just ridiculous. We're not children.

*This moment. Then she is looking down at her clenched fists. And, to break the
moment*

Rose Well I'm starting if no-one else is. (*She faces the mirror and starts the
warm-up routine*)
Vera We'd better do something I suppose.
Dorothy Suppose—yes.

Dorothy and Vera and then Maxine join in and Geoffrey hovers

Sylvia Are you all right, love?
Andy Why can't people ...
Sylvia (*holding up her hand*) Sorry, sorry ...

*She moves to join in with the others ... and Andy glances up to see Geoffrey
looking at her ... then he is moving to the piano, lifting the lid, and begins to
play—"The Entertainer"*

Attaboy Geoffrey.

*Then suddenly Geoffrey changes the tempo ... playing accomplished and
unfettered boogie-woogie ... and they react with delight ... Sylvia moving
round to squeeze his head against her ample bosom ... and they are all dancing
in their own free-form way as*

*Mavis and Mrs Fraser enter. Mavis wears a velour tracksuit and carries her
canvas bag and Mrs Fraser's music case. Mrs Fraser carries her voluminous
bag*

Mavis (*above the noise of the piano and dancing*) Sorry to keep you everyone
... traffic ...

*Mrs Fraser moves quickly across to glare down at Geoffrey who hasn't seen
them arrive. Now he sees her and stops playing and eases away from the piano
as Mavis sits next to the piano and quickly ties on her tap shoes ... and Mrs
Fraser looks at the piano keys as though examining them for damage and will
sort out her music. This as*

We'll do the full hour I promise you—anyway—(*she smiles up at them*)—
you don't seem to have been wasting your time.

Sylvia You know us, Mavis, dead keen.

Maxine We thought you'd deserted us.

Mavis Now would I do a thing like that?

Vera (*hand up, moving forward*) Would you like me to do the register,
Mavis?

Mavis Oh, I think we'll leave that until later, don't you?

Mrs Fraser Just as long as we remember.

Geoffrey (*handing Mavis the hall key*) The hall key, um, Mavis.

Mavis Thank you Geoffrey—right—you've done the warm-up I take it?

General murmuring of assent

OK, so what we'll do is run straight into the piece we started last week.

Sylvia Great. What piece we started last week?

Dorothy You remember—it's ... (*She demonstrates with her usual extrava-
gance*)

Sylvia Oh. That piece. I thought you meant the other piece.

Maxine What other piece?

Sylvia strikes a pose as if to start, but

Sylvia I forget.

Mavis So it's ... (*she demonstrates a group of steps, chanting the rhythm. See
Dance Notes p. 79*) ... OK?

They move into their lines, Vera taking up a place in the front row

All right Glenda? And it's five six seven eight ...

*Mrs Fraser begins to play—"I Got Rhythm"—at a regulation tempo ... and
they dance ... with Mavis calling out the steps and, as they dance ...*

The Lights change suddenly to blue and all the dancers freeze ...

*Mrs Fraser continues to play ... the tempo of her playing changing so that it
becomes faster, and*

The Lights come up again and the class resumes dancing, and it is

SCENE 3

*A month later. The class, led by Mavis, is coming to the end of a spirited tap
routine. They are generally a little more competent and are putting steps
together, making up the routine as Mavis calls out the steps and smiles
encouragement. The session has been a good one and they are all enjoying it.
The dancing comes to a well-synchronized end*

Mavis Well done everyone, that was really good, yes?

*She is patting her chest and sounding more breathless than she perhaps really
is. Several of the class are genuinely breathless but all are well-pleased with
themselves, some whooping with pleasure as Dorothy puts up her hand*

Dorothy Was I all right in the middle bit, Mavis?

Mavis Much better—but it still needs to be that little bit smaller—(*she demonstrates as*)—not so much work—nice and relaxed—yes?

Dorothy Relaxed—yes.

Mavis Rose—you're still not quite getting the scissors. It's . . . (*she demonstrates*) . . . yes?

Rose The thing is, I don't really see myself as a scissors person.

Mavis Well keep trying, you never know. Lynne—it's—(*she demonstrates*)—yes?

Lynne repeats the step

Lynne Oh yes, I was forgetting the . . . (*She does the step she was missing out*)

Mavis So you've got it now—sure? Sylvia . . . (*she demonstrates*) . . . you're still starting off on the same foot.

Sylvia Yeah I know, it's chronic.

Mavis Any idea what the problem is?

Sylvia No. I just seem to use whatever foot comes to hand.

Mavis Anyone else got any problems? Maxine? Anyone else? No? OK, that's it for tonight then, we'll pick it up from there next week and once again well done everyone, you can be really pleased with yourselves—thank you.

Immediately, Mrs Fraser plays a piano roll which continues as the class takes a bow and then breaks up, applauding Mavis as is the custom at the end of a session. Mrs Fraser instantly starts putting her music away as Maxine does a flashy little step

Maxine Look, ma, I'm dancing!

Sylvia Wayne Sleep, eat your heart out.

She does a little clod-hopping routine and she and Maxine finish together with the stamp-stamp hands out position of "How's that?"

Rose Wayne Sleep? Now there is a lovely little man and no mistaking.

Sylvia You like 'em small, do you Rosie?

Maxine So do I darling, but not that small.

Lynne (*to Dorothy*) Do you like small men?

Dorothy I don't really think about it.

Rose Small is beautiful.

Sylvia No, it's your big ones I go for, your tall ones, your James Coburns, you know what I mean?

Rose Big men is a fallacy.

Sylvia It's the way they look down on you.

Maxine Like Hampstead.

They change their clothing . . . and Dorothy and Lynne practise a step, mainly for Dorothy's benefit . . . and Vera bustles around, humming the tune they've just danced to, putting various debris—including two cans of orange juice and a banana skin from the piano—into a wastebin . . . and Mrs Fraser collects up her things and reads her magazine . . . Mavis sits a little wearily and lights a cigarette . . . and Andy moves to Lynne and Dorothy, getting signatures for a petition ... all this as Vera makes to empty Mavis' ashtray but Mavis indicates that she's still using it

Vera I hope you don't mind my asking, Mavis, but have you ever tried to stop smoking?

Mavis Yes I did once but I got bad tempered and I ate too much and I put on weight and I had to buy new clothes and I upset my fella and I've got enough hassle without all that ... so ... I smoke. (*She smiles up at Vera*)

Vera makes to move away but sees a disgusting-looking sock hanging over the back of a chair and takes it up between finger and thumb and continues into the changing room

Andy moves to Maxine to get her signature but Maxine takes up a package and gives it to Mavis

Maxine I nearly forgot: those T-shirts I promised you.

Mavis Oh—lovely—how much do I owe you?

Maxine No hurry—have a look at them first, you might not like the colour, I could only get the blue.

Mavis You're sure?

Maxine Sure I'm sure, see me next week.

She moves away. Mrs Fraser has been eyeing this exchange grimly

Mrs Fraser It should be you doing the selling, not her.

Andy (*generally*) Would anyone else like to sign the petition?

Rose What petition?

Andy About the common.

Sylvia What about it?

Andy (*generally, awkwardly*) In the event of a nuclear war, they're designating it as a mass burial ground.

Rose Who is they?

Andy The council—I do have some literature if anyone's interested.

Maxine Andy's very active in these matters.

Andy Yes, well, I do think it's necessary to ...

Maxine She's on the protest committee.

Rose The thing is, Andy, what exactly are you protesting about?

Andy Well, as I say, the use of the common as a mass burial ground—or rather, the proposed designation without prior consultation.

Rose (*moving to the changing room*) Oh I can't worry about that—I got enough to think about with my hop shuffle step turn shuffle.

Andy Yes, but unless we do something ...

Rose What does it matter where they put us?

She goes into the changing room

Sylvia I betcha if they do drop it, they drop it on a Monday. Just after I've hung my washing out.

Dorothy Mavis will be pleased anyway—it'll be the first time we're all together.

Mavis smiles as she goes into the changing room

Sylvia Come on then Andy, give it here.

Sylvia signs the petition as Dorothy and Lynne make to go into the changing room, Dorothy taking up her handbag

Dorothy You're ever so good, Lynne, you could have been a professional.
Lynne Well I did think about it . . . but I got too tall.

They go into the changing room as Vera comes out with

Vera Has anyone seen a little gold belt?
Maxine (*holding up a belt from a chair*) Is this it?
Vera Oh there it is, thankseversomuch Maxine.
Andy If anyone's interested, there's a meeting on the common this Saturday.
Vera I'm going to a wedding this Saturday.
Maxine Anyone you know?
Vera Lionel's cousin. It's going to be ever such a smart do—they're having a marquee. I like weddings, don't you?
Sylvia Not a lot.
Vera Mine was lovely I must say.
Sylvia Mine was quite boring actually. I'm sorry I went.
Vera I can remember every detail of mine.
Sylvia So can I.
Vera Can you, Maxine?
Maxine When it comes to my weddings—instant recoil, darling, instant recoil.
Vera Oh. Have you been married a lot then?
Maxine Just the twice, Vera, don't get excited.
Vera I didn't know you'd been married before, Maxine.
Sylvia You do like to keep abreast, don't you, Vera?
Vera No, I'm just saying.
Maxine I'll send you the cuttings. (*To Andy, of the petition*) Let's have a look, darling.
Vera Of course, the thing about divorce, it's the children that really suffer, isn't it?
Maxine What did I need children for, I had him.
Sylvia One of those, was he?

Mavis comes out of the changing room

Mavis Has anyone not paid yet?
Mrs Fraser (*not looking up from her reading*) Sylvia.
Mavis Would you mind, Sylvia—sorry. (*To Mrs Fraser*) Anyone else?
Mrs Fraser Just Sylvia and she didn't pay last week if you care to remember.
Maxine What really finished me was the day I came home and found him admiring this set of love bites on his neck. Another woman I might have coped with but these were self-inflicted.

Sylvia has taken her money to Mavis

Mavis Sorry Sylvia, but I do have to keep the books straight.

Sylvia You should ask Rose—she's a bookkeeper. I owe you for last week an'all.

Vera But you're happy now, are you? You don't mind my asking, do you?

Maxine Happy, what's happy? You pretend to be happy, sometimes you end up happy. I'd be a lot happier if someone could tell me how to bring up step-children.

Andy I wonder if it takes as much courage to live alone as it does to live with someone else?

They look at her

Rose comes out of the changing room with her bag

Vera Did I hear someone say you were a bookkeeper, Rose?

Rose That's right, Vera: I am the financial genius behind Mr Patel's entire filing cabinet.

Vera Oh yes?

She continues into the changing room

Sylvia She must have ears in the back of her tights.

Maxine You girls going for a drink then?

Sylvia We thought we'd give this new wine bar a whirl, yeah.

Maxine Only I thought I might join you.

Sylvia Why not, the more the merrier—how about you, Mavis, fancy a drink?

Maxine takes a brush from her bag and titivates in the practice mirror

Mavis Not tonight thanks, I've got to get back. (*She collects up her things*)

Sylvia Keeps you on a tight rein, does he?

Mrs Fraser (*to herself*) He's never there.

Maxine I quite fancy a drink tonight. Wonderboy's got the house full of yobboes. God alone know what's happening to my Dralon. Yeah, why not—let his father deal with it for a change.

Rose Geoffrey?

Geoffrey I've got some work to catch up on, I'm afraid.

Sylvia Come on, Geoffrey, come and help me spend the old man's ill-gotten.

Geoffrey No, not this week, really.

Mrs Fraser Don't anyone ask me.

Maxine How about you, Mrs Fraser?

Mrs Fraser I don't go to public houses thankyouverymuch.

Rose Come on, Mrs F, come and have a giggle.

Sylvia Anyway it's not a public house it's a wine bar.

Mrs Fraser I don't drink.

Sylvia You must drink, Mrs Fraser, otherwise your liver gets all bunged up.

Mrs Fraser I'm referring to alcohol.

Maxine Is that because you're a vegetarian?

Mrs Fraser That does enter into it, certainly.

Sylvia Well we can have a drink and you can chew a carrot.

Vera comes out of the changing room, dressed ready to leave

Vera I haven't done the ashtrays, Mavis.
Sylvia Oh my gawd Vera hasn't done the ashtrays.
Mavis Don't worry, I'll do them.
Vera We're not the only ones who use this place, you know.
Maxine I hope not, there's a jock-strap hanging up out there.
Rose I like your coat, Vera.
Vera Do you? It's ever so old.
Rose Lovely material.
Vera Yes I know, that's why I thought I'd alter it. I'm quite pleased really.

Dorothy and Lynne come out of the changing room, Dorothy with her bicycle basket etc. and call out their good-nights as they go out

Andy takes up her petition and moves to Mavis

Andy Would you mind, Mavis, you did say . . .
Mavis No of course I don't mind. (*She signs the petition*)

Geoffrey takes the opportunity of making a discreet exit . . . calling out his good-nights

They adlib their good-nights to him . . . Andy's being somewhat louder than the others. Andy offers the petition to Mrs Fraser

Mrs Fraser I don't sign petitions, thank you.

Vera has sat to check her hair and make-up. Maxine nudges Rose and, somewhat unwillingly

Maxine Coming for a drink, Vera?
Vera No I don't think so thank you, I'm not dressed or anything.
Sylvia It's only a wine bar.
Vera Yes I know but I couldn't, not like this.
Sylvia Like what?
Vera My hair and everything—besides, I'm all sweaty.
Sylvia Well I'm not sweaty.
Vera It may be February outside but it's always August under your armpits.
Sylvia Well that's charming I must say.
Vera Not being funny but it's true though, isn't it? Besides, Lionel might be phoning from Stuttgart. Bye Mavis see you next week, bye everybody have a lovely weekend.

She goes out briskly

Sylvia It's bleeding April anyway.

They make to go out, but Sylvia remembers

Here, Andy—fancy coming for a drink?
Andy appears totally thrown

Andy Oh dear . . . um . . . no I can't actually . . . but thank you.
Sylvia Some other time then.

She and Rose and Maxine are already on their way out, ad libbing their good-nights . . . and they go off

Andy hovers. Mavis becomes aware of her

Mavis Yes Andy.
Andy I just wanted to say that I . . . felt better tonight. I really felt I was . . . what I mean is, I felt more relaxed . . . I mean, I know I'm not very good but . . .
Mavis Why do you come to these classes, Andy?
Andy Why?
Mavis Why do you come? What do you get out of it?
Andy I come because . . . (*she hesitates but decides on the truth*) . . . I come because it's the only thing in the week I do for me. Everything else is for other people.
Mavis And d'you know what I get out of it? Seeing people enjoying themselves. Oh sure, I like to see you all improving, it's good for you, it's good for me. But the biggest buzz—the real buzz—is enjoying ourselves. Yes?

She smiles. And after a moment, Andy smiles

Andy Good-night.
Mavis Good-night, Andy.

Andy goes out

Mrs Fraser You should be selling encyclopaedias.
Mavis I've done it.
Mrs Fraser There's not much you haven't done really, is there?
Mavis If I don't sell these classes, we'd both be out of a job, wouldn't we?
Mrs Fraser I don't think you need worry about me.
Mavis I'm not worrying about you, Glenda, I'm just reminding you.
Mrs Fraser In my opinion it's about time that so-called man of yours got himself a job.

Mavis ignores this and wearily moves round, straightening chairs etc

I suppose you know she gives him a lift home.
Mavis Gives who a lift home?
Mrs Fraser Geoffrey, who d'you think?
Mavis Andy, you mean?
Mrs Fraser That's right, Andy.
Mavis So she gives him a lift home, so what?
Mrs Fraser Always the quiet ones.
Mavis You're a wicked old bird at times.
Mrs Fraser We'll see.

Mavis sits to take off her tap shoes

You look tired out.
Mavis I feel tired—OK?
Mrs Fraser You do too much.
Mavis Do I.
Mrs Fraser Running around, wasting your life—and for what?
Mavis Mind your own bloody business.
Mrs Fraser (*smugly*) I see.
Mavis My life—all right?
Mrs Fraser (*still smug*) Since you were that high.
Mavis (*pulling on her coat*) Yeah, yeah, yeah, I'm very grateful and I always will be grateful but that doesn't give you the right to ... you go too far, Glenda ... sometimes you go too far. (*She takes up her bag and moves to the door, and without looking back*) Are you coming or aren't you?

She goes out

A moment. Then Mrs Fraser goes unhurriedly to the door. As she reaches up to turn off the light, the Lights go to Black-out

The sound of "Happy Feet" comes up which continues and then stops suddenly and the Lights come up for the next scene

SCENE 4

The same. A month later. 7.40 p.m.

Mavis, in her tracksuit, is alone in the room. She stands, C, leaning down to consult her exercise book which is on the floor. She takes a puff of her cigarette then puts it down and, looking at herself in the mirror, goes through the combination of steps she will teach this evening. She taps perfunctorily, then stops. She remains looking at herself in the mirror ... and then smiles at some sudden thought and begins to dance again ... this time a much more complicated routine. She dances freely, enjoying herself, caught up at what is really a tap down memory lane

As she dances, Lynne enters. She wears her blue nurse's raincoat, carries her bag. Seeing Mavis, she stands quietly by the door, watching

Mavis, unaware, continues to dance—and the steps carry her round and for the first time she becomes aware of Lynne and is startled and immediately stops dancing

Mavis God you gave me a fright. (*It's an over-reaction at being caught off-guard like this. She takes up her cigarette*)
Lynne I'm sorry, I didn't mean to ...
Mavis No, don't be silly, you made me jump, that's all.
Lynne Sorry.
Mavis I was just going through the stuff for tonight. Trying to keep one step ahead of you lot.

She smiles at Lynne. A moment

Lynne I wish I could dance like that.
Mavis You will.
Lynne No. Not really. There's a difference, isn't there?
Mavis I've been doing it for years, don't forget.
Lynne No, but there is. There's a difference.

She moves to put down her bag in front of the stage. Mavis stubs out her cigarette, turns to look at her

Mavis You all right, Lynne? You look a bit miz—not like my Lynne.

Lynne attempts a smile as if to say "I'm OK", but

Lynne One of my old ladies died this morning. I'm in geriatric this week and—well, to be honest, it's the first patient I've seen die. I didn't realize I'd be so upset, fine nurse I am, aren't I? I suppose what really upset me was—well, nobody ever came to see her. And all last night she was trying to talk to me but . . . we were so busy. Sometimes it's really quiet but last night we were . . . so busy.
Mavis I'm sorry.
Lynne I'll have to get used to it, won't I? And I will, of course I will. Which is somehow worse in a way, isn't it? (*She changes the subject brightly*) Did you always want to be a dancer?
Mavis Did I always want to be a dancer. Yes. Yes I suppose I did really.
Lynne You must have been really good.
Mavis Not bad.
Lynne D'you miss it?
Mavis (*smiling*) You mean why did I give it up. There wasn't the work. Not for me there wasn't anyway. It's an over-crowded profession, the union's hopeless and chorus girls of "a certain age" don't come too high on the shopping list. (*She takes up another cigarette but doesn't quite get round to lighting it as*) Anyway, I was already phasing out—I'd started up a little business with a friend—jewellery, making jewellery—and the business started taking off and then my friend took off but that's another story and someone said why don't you start a class which seemed like a good idea as any—oh, I enjoy teaching, it gives me a real buzz I promise you and you girls are great, really great, I really look forward to these classes.
Lynne Did you do any big shows?
Mavis A few. In the chorus. I did understudy the lead a couple of times but never went on—nearly, but not quite. It's the morning you wake up and realize you have no more expectations. That's when you make the big decision. So . . . I made it. (*She is finally lighting the cigarette as*)

Maxine comes in

Maxine Evening Mavis how's Mavis, hello Lynne how's Lynne? I have had a day you wouldn't believe, believe me.

Dorothy comes in

Hello Dorothy how's Dorothy?
Dorothy Is it all right if I bring my bike in, Mavis, someone tried to steal it

today and I'm a bit nervous.
Mavis Oh dear—yes of course.

Dorothy ducks out again and Lynne goes to help her

Maxine First of all the wholesaler lets me down, then I have to go and see
my solicitor and when I come out I've got one of those clamp things on
my wheel. Three hours it takes me, you wouldn't believe those people.

Lynne holds open the doors and Dorothy awkwardly wheels in her bicycle

Dorothy Will it be all right here, Mavis?
Mavis Fine.
Dorothy I don't think it will interfere with anything.

With the help of Lynne she leans it against the front of the stage

Mavis No, that's fine.
Dorothy Fine—yes.

She takes the basket from the bicycle and goes into the changing room

Maxine So I finally crawl home and the neighbours start on me. Wonderboy's been firing his airgun out of the bedroom window and this Cypriot
next door is complaining he's knocked the eye out of one of his lions. He's
got these two stone lions on the front wall. The whole street is ashamed.
Two stone lions and the family crest above the garage—(*she indicates*)—
"I Live To Serve". We all know he lives to serve, he runs a fish and chip
shop. He calls it a seafood restaurant, but it's a fish and chip shop, believe
me.

Mrs Fraser comes in with her bag and music case

Mrs Fraser What's a bicycle doing in here?
Lynne It's Dorothy's.

Mrs Fraser moves to the piano

Mrs Fraser I see: a bicycle shed now, is it?
Maxine It may be a bicycle shed to you, Mrs Fraser, but to me it's an oasis.
Mrs Fraser Oh yes? (*To Mavis*) You didn't bring the car then.
Mavis Sorry?
Mrs Fraser The car's not outside.
Mavis No, I lent it to Sean.
Mrs Fraser What's wrong with his own car or has he sold it again?
Mavis Don't worry, he's bringing it back, you'll get your lift home.
Mrs Fraser Last thought on my mind.

*Geoffrey comes in. He makes for his usual chair at the front of the stage and
is somewhat thrown to find a bicycle there. This as*

Maxine moves to pay Mavis

Maxine Then his father comes home in one of his moods—he's had a bad
day—*you've* had a bad day? When I tell him about Wonderboy on safari,
he doesn't even know he's got an airgun. "Why didn't you stop him

buying it," he says. "Have I ever been able to stop him doing anything? He's eighteen years old, he's not my son, he's your son and whenever I do try talking to him all I get is stop nagging you're not even my own mother." Kids. I love'em. I can't have'em but I love'em.

Rose and Sylvia enter cheerily with their bags

Sylvia Hello, someone's left a bike.
Maxine It's Dorothy's.
Sylvia Pity—I could've done with a nice bike.
Rose You told me you were having driving lessons.
Sylvia Contemplating driving lessons.
Geoffrey Why has she brought it inside?
Sylvia Like I'm contemplating a house in Bermuda.

Vera bustles in

Vera Hello everyone sorry I'm late.
Sylvia You're not late.
Vera I nearly didn't make it this evening, actually.

She moves straight into the changing room

Geoffrey Has something happened then?
Rose Perhaps Lionel was phoning from Stuttgart.
Geoffrey I mean Dorothy.

Throughout this, they each move to pay Mrs Fraser

Lynne She nearly had it stolen today so she's a bit nervous.

Dorothy comes out of the changing room, changed, with her handbag

Andy comes in and moves to speak quietly to Mavis

Sylvia Is that right, Dorothy, someone tried to nick your bike?
Dorothy Bike—yes, I know—it had the chain on and everything.
Mavis (*going towards the entrance lobby*) Won't be a sec, everyone—just got to take a phone call.

Mavis goes out

Andy and Geoffrey exchange their little smiles

Rose Both my boys had theirs taken last year.
Dorothy I depend on my bicycle—well you do, don't you?
Rose Go to the police—what happens—nothing.
Dorothy Nothing—no.
Geoffrey I think it's about a thousand a day in London.
Sylvia Oh yeah?
Geoffrey Most of them get shipped over to the continent. They're twice as expensive over there—so if you steal, say, five a day and sell them for just twenty pounds each ...
Sylvia That's five hundred a week.
Maxine And no overheads.

Sylvia I'll have a word with my Terry.

Geoffrey Most of it's well-organized: it isn't just random theft.

Sylvia Oh I wouldn't like him to thieve at random. I'd like him to be organized. In fact I'd insist on it.

They put on their tap shoes etc. as

Vera comes out of the changing room. She is wearing a tight silver catsuit

Rose Hey—look at Vera.

Vera D'you like it? (*She is admiring herself in the mirror*)

General murmurings of approval from the women

Rose That is really something.

Sylvia Perhaps she'll make you one.

Vera Oh I didn't make it, not this. I was in town so I popped into Pineapple.

Dorothy (*to Sylvia, it's been worrying her*) Your husband wouldn't really steal bicycles, would he?

Sylvia Leave it out, Dorothy.

Vera It was ever so expensive but I simply couldn't resist it. D'you like it, Maxine?

Maxine It's very nice.

Vera (*pushing out her breasts*) It's not too bold, is it?

Mrs Fraser I'd be very careful about wearing it to Ascot.

Maxine Oh I don't know: every crowd needs a silver lining.

Vera I thought it might be a bit bold.

Rose What we need is the man's opinion. Geoffrey—is that too bold or is that too bold?

Vera poses for him

Geoffrey Umm ... no, it's ... er ...

Sylvia You cannot say fairer than that.

Rose Thank you Geoffrey.

Dorothy The thing is, if he's tried it before, he could try it again, couldn't he?

Sylvia Don't worry about it, Dorothy.

Dorothy Yes, but I need it to get to the office.

Sylvia Where d'you work then?

Dorothy Hadley House.

Sylvia That name rings a bell.

Mrs Fraser (*to herself*) I'm not surprised.

Rose Hadley House? That's the social security place.

Sylvia Course it is—here—d'you work for the social security, Dorothy?

Dorothy I do, yes.

Sylvia I've never met anyone who works for the social security—all the people I know are working against it.

Rose Don't embarrass the woman.

Dorothy I'm not embarrassed, why should I be embarrassed?

Mrs Fraser Has anyone not yet paid?

Sylvia (*putting up her hand*) Just coming, miss, promise. Here, Rose, lend us a couple.

Rose gives her the money and Sylvia pays Mrs Fraser

Vera I like your top, Maxine, it's lovely.
Maxine How much, d'you reckon?
Vera I don't know, it must have cost a fortune.
Maxine Five quid.
Vera Where?
Maxine This woman I go to in Hampstead—she's got some beautiful stuff, really beautiful.
Vera Seriously—five pounds?
Maxine Never been worn. You know some of these women, they buy something, change their mind, wear it just once maybe . . .
Vera You mean second-hand.
Maxine Second-hand, nearly-new, call it what you like. If you're interested, next time I go, I'll take you.
Vera Oh no I couldn't. No. Not second-hand. (*She flutters a hand at Rose*) Hello Rose.

She moves away. Sylvia has been regarding herself in the mirror

Sylvia What's another word for grotesque?
Rose Think positive.
Sylvia Right. You are positively grotesque.
Rose (*to Maxine*) How is he behaving himself?
Maxine He's all right, we're very pleased with him.
Rose His father want me to say . . . if he give you any trouble——
Maxine If he gives me any trouble, he's out. (*She puts her arm fondly around Rose's shoulder.*) Stop worrying, he's doing all right, I promise you.

Vera taps her way to Andy who is wearing a long cardigan over her leotard, so that they are both looking into the mirror, downstage, as

Vera I hope you don't mind my asking, Andy, but why do you always cover yourself up?

Andy instinctively touches her upper arm

Andy Why do I what?
Vera What I mean is—you've got a nice body in its own way.
Andy Really.
Vera Really. It's long, but it's nice. It seems such a pity to cover it up all the time.
Andy Perhaps I should pop into Pineapple and find something more suitable.
Vera I wish I'd mentioned it before, we could have gone together.
Andy I think you're being rather rude, don't you?
Vera I wasn't trying to be nosey or anything . . .
Andy There's nothing to be nosey about. I wear what I want to wear. Sorry, Vera.

She moves away and sees that Geoffrey has been watching this exchange

Mavis comes in and goes straight up on to the stage

Mavis Right ladies—Geoffrey—if I can just have your attention please.
Sylvia Oo-er that sounds nasty.

They turn to look at her

Mavis Liz Beckley has just phoned me—she runs the local ILEA classes—
some of you probably know her, yes?
Vera (*hand up*) Yes.
Mavis Well anyway, she's been asked to get together a charity show for the
end of July—all the local dance groups will be taking part and she's very
keen for us to do the tap number. I said I'd speak to you but I'm pretty
sure the answer will be yes.

General murmurings. Mrs Fraser even manages to look up from her magazine

So then—what do you think?

They seem stunned into silence

Rose For the end of July.
Mavis Plenty of time I promise you.
Vera What sort of thing would we have to do then?
Mavis The same sort of thing we're doing now.
Sylvia Oh my gawd.
Andy (*putting up her hand*) You'd want us all to be in it, would you?
Mavis Only if you want to be. Anyone who doesn't, doesn't have to—all I
ask is that you let me know because obviously I'll have to work out some
sort of routine.
Dorothy What charity is it?
Mavis Save The Children.
Maxine Wouldn't you know it?
Geoffrey (*hand up*) When you say you'll work out some sort of routine,
umm . . .
Mavis It won't be anything more difficult than we've already done—you've
learned to tap so let's put it together and really show them what we can
do, yes?
Vera Anyway, it's only for charity, isn't it?
Dorothy Charity—yes.
Andy Yes, I mean . . . they won't expect much, will they?
Mavis Now hold on ladies . . . that's the wrong attitude. As far as I'm
concerned, being asked is—well, it's something of an honour and what
they're going to get is the best we can give them. Anyway, have a think
about it and if any of you are really unhappy, let me know next week,
OK?
Maxine Well I think it's a great idea. I would have preferred to save the
parents, but . . .

The others join in with her enthusiasm

Sylvia I'll give it a whirl, yeah, why not?

Lynne It'll be fun, won't it?
Dorothy We're really going to sock it to them, aren't we Mavis?
Sylvia Here, listen to her all of a sudden.
Mavis No, but she's right, absolutely right.
Dorothy Right—yes.
Mavis Let them know what we've been doing every Thursday—yes?

General murmurings, more enthusiastic still

OK, that's enough of that, have a think about it and we'll move on ...

They talk amongst themselves, some doing fancy steps to show how good they'll be on the night, as

What we'll do is go right in where we finished last week, yes? (*To Mrs Fraser*) "Let's Face The Music and Dance".
Mrs Fraser I should have been told about this.
Mavis I've only just found out about it myself.
Mrs Fraser Nevertheless I should have been consulted.
Mavis (*clapping her hands*) OK everyone, let's have you in two lines ...

They form up

Mrs Fraser (*a sudden fierce announcement*) I don't suppose that any of you know, and I don't suppose that any of you care, but today is Irving Berlin's birthday and I for one do not intend to let the occasion pass without tribute.

She plays and sings a spirited version of "Happy Birthday to You ... Happy Birthday to You ... Happy Birthday Dear Irving, Happy Birthday To-oo You". She stops playing. They have listened in stunned silence. A moment

Dorothy It's my birthday next Tuesday.
Mrs Fraser Are you starting or what?
Mavis Whenever you're ready, Glenda ... and five six seven eight ...

Mrs Fraser plays a snappy version of "Let's Face The Music and Dance" ... and they dance (See Dance Notes p. 79) ... and Mavis turns out front, dancing with them ... so that they are all dancing and smiling happily and some of them join in with singing the words of the song as it comes to an end and they stop dancing, holding this pose, arms outstretched, smiling, facing the audience ...

The Lights go quickly to Black-out as the sound of the orchestrated version of "Let's Face The Music And Dance" comes up, which continues as

the CURTAIN *falls*

ACT II

The same. A week later, May

Mrs Fraser stands po-faced, watching Mavis supervising Geoffrey who is pushing the piano further back upstage. The class members stand around chatting. Rose no longer wears the wig. Her hair is short and curly. Lynne is going round with the cashbox, collecting subs. Dorothy is wearing a pair of handknitted legwarmers and a matching headband. She sits next to Andy, fussing with the legwarmers

Dorothy I mean, it's not her fault she's an invalid, is it, Andy?

Andy No of course it isn't.

Dorothy Isn't—no. She is his mother as well as mine, you'd think he'd want to help out, wouldn't you?

Andy I'm afraid people can be . . .

Dorothy Very selfish—yes.

Vera takes up the wastebin

Maxine (*of Rose's hair*) It's growing out very nicely.

Rose I don't like it.

Maxine No, it suits you—doesn't it, Geoffrey?

Geoffrey Sorry?

Maxine Rose's hair—it suits her.

Geoffrey Yes, it's very—umm . . .

Dorothy And he can be so hurtful. It's all right for you, he says, you're not married. I know I'm not married but I'm entitled to some sort of life, aren't I? I mean, one night a week I get off and even then he doesn't offer, I have to pay a sitter, I don't know, it's so unfair.

Vera has been busying around with her wastebin and pauses at Sylvia who sits in front of the mirror, on the floor, activating her outstretched thighs

Vera *I* used to be fat, you know.

Sylvia (*looking up slowly*) Oh yes?

Vera Mmm. Just after I had my baby. I was nearly as big as you are.

Sylvia Well well.

Vera She's seventeen now. All she thinks about is horses, horse-mad she is.

Sylvia Well, keep her off the streets, won't it?

Vera moves away

Dorothy (*holding up a leg*) D'you like my new legwarmers, Rose? They go with my headband.

Rose (*flatly*) Very nice, Dorothy.
Dorothy They're my birthday present from Vera.
Maxine Here, Andy—we went to see that play you recommendea.
Andy Oh—yes—did you enjoy it?
Maxine What can I say? We didn't even understand the interval.
Mavis OK everyone, let's get on, shall we? It's our first rehearsal, so lots of concentration, yes?

They pay attention and Mrs Frazer takes up her magazine to read. This is the first rehearsal for the show and some of them are looking forward to it and some are apprehensive. Mavis' attitude will be a touch brisker—more "professional". They're amateurs, she's aware of their limitations, but it's a show and her name is on it

(*Indicating*) Rose, Sylvia and Andy—we'll take you three at the back— no, Rose in the middle please—then we'll have Maxine, Vera, Lynne and Dorothy—spread yourselves out so you can be seen—but come forward a step, you're crowding—and Geoffrey, let's have you at the front, directly in front of Rose.
Sylvia Shame.

Mavis moves among them, checking that each is in the right position and moves to the front

Mavis OK. So you're standing with your backs to the audience ... (*she demonstrates, turning her back to them*) ... feet apart and absolutely perfectly still—nothing moving. The curtains or the lights come up or whatever and you stay there, not moving, absolutely static still. For four counts you do absolutely nothing.
Rose I like it.

As Mavis demonstrates the following steps, they attempt to join in with varying degrees of efficiency

Mavis On given counts, back line, middle line and Geoffrey turn round and face the front ... no, you don't move your feet and so your legs are crossed ...

They cross their legs, most of them unbalanced

From there you bring the right arm up, leaving the left arm down, you lift the hat and you hold it high—yes?
Andy (*anxiously to Rose*) Are we having hats? I didn't hear her say anything about hats ...
Mavis That's the first two counts, yes? On counts three and four——
Mrs Fraser (*still reading*) You're forgetting the sticks
Mavis (*who most certainly had*) Yes, you're right, thank you Glenda ... (*generally*) ... sorry, sorry, I've forgotten the sticks.
Mrs Fraser Forget your head one of these days. (*She licks a thumb, turns a page*)
Andy Are we having sticks?
Mavis So ... (*she demonstrates*) ... you're not standing with the left arm

down, you're standing with the stick under your arm ... you turn ... and up with the right arm.

Lynne (*trying it*) Stick under the arm, up with the hat.

Mavis On counts three and four, middle line of four does exactly the same thing but when you turn you leave the right arm down, holding the hat low.

Lynne Sorry.

Mavis So you've got the contrast between the back line being high and the middle line being low, and Geoffrey—who is on his own as a solo—is high, yes?

Some of them try the hat and stick movements as

Maxine Can I ask a question?

Mavis Yes Maxine.

Maxine What do you mean—a solo?

Mavis You mean Geoffrey?

Vera Do you mean he's going to be special or something? Not being funny or anything, Geoffrey ...

Geoffrey No, no, I was wondering myself what ...

Mavis Geoffrey's going to be special inasmuch as he's a guy and sticks out like a sore thumb but his solo part is going to be positional rather than a lot of tapping—yes?

Vera Oh I see.

Maxine Got you.

Rose Excuse me.

Mavis Yes Rose.

Rose I can think of someone else who'll stick out like a sore thumb.

Mavis (*grinning*) Ah ... I wondered when ...

Rose Don't worry—I see myself as the token spade, there's always a token spade, right?

Mavis (*still smiling*) Something like that, Rose, I must admit.

Andy (*hand up*) I wonder then if Rose shouldn't be at the front with Geoffrey?

Geoffrey Or I'd be quite happy to change places if ...

Rose No, no, Geoffrey—if I'm going to be ignored, I prefer to be ignored at the back, thanks all the same.

Mavis Going back to the Geoffrey business ... it's a big heavy tap number, yes—you're working as a team, there's no individuality—apart from one section where each of you in turn will move across and do a step while the others are marking time—but because you're doing a step on your own, it doesn't mean that you're the superstar—there's no big solo spot, it's a team.

Sylvia Did you say do a step on our own?

Mavis Right.

Sylvia Thought so.

Mavis No-one's going to look silly, I promise you. You'll do what I know you can do—and they'll think it's wonderful, believe me.

Vera We'll all be wearing the same costume then, will we?

Mavis Oh yes, I think so, don't you?
Dorothy (*to Lynne*) It's quite exciting, isn't it?
Maxine What sort of costume are we talking about?
Andy We can discuss that later, surely?
Dorothy Later—yes.
Maxine I might be able to help, that's all.

Mrs Fraser loudly clears her throat

Vera Actually, I could probably make something.
Maxine Whatever—I don't mind.
Vera As long as we decide so I've got time.
Mavis OK we'll discuss it later and you can choose whatever you'll feel happiest in.
Sylvia (*demonstrating*) How about a nice big plastic bag?
Maxine The hats I can definitely get—(*she looks pointedly at Andy*)—sorry to mention it, Andy.
Mavis That's good, yes, thank you.
Maxine The sticks—I don't think so.
Lynne Will we be getting some sticks, Mavis? I mean to practice with.
Dorothy Practice with—yes.
Andy (*hand up*) If we're going to have a stick, I think I'd like to get used to it as soon as possible.
Dorothy As soon as possible—yes.
Mavis Absolutely—the sooner the better—so if you could bring one in please—OK, let's move on, shall we? So ...
Vera Are they special sticks or what? Sorry.
Mavis Go to a garden centre, buy yourself a cane and cut it down, yes?
Andy (*hand up*) Does that mean for this week we umm ...
Maxine Pretend, darling—like you do with your husband, go through the motions and make like you're enjoying it.
Mavis (*going up on the stage*) Incidentally, there's going to be some fast bouncing around and you might have bust troubles so wear something good and firm, yes?

They all look down at their busts. Geoffrey nods wisely

(*To Mrs Fraser*) I want four bars of solid intro and then——
Mrs Fraser Hats and sticks? You're asking for trouble.
Mavis (*generally*) Right—we'll have the first four bars and make sure the intro is spot on—it's got to be good, it's got to have panache, it's got to have the three T's—what are the three T's? Tits, teeth and tonsils ... (*she demonstrates*) ... you smile, you stick your chest out, you look like you're enjoying it.
Rose You've only got two T's, haven't you, Geoffrey?
Sylvia Don't worry, Geoffrey, I've got plenty, you can have some of mine.
Mavis Let's have you in your positions ... (*She moves amongst them, checking*) Knees straight, everything tidy, perfectly still. When you turn round, the movement has got to be clean sharp and absolutely hold it

once you've got there . . . and once you're there, you keep holding it, you
don't move a muscle.

Sylvia My Terry'd be good at this.

Mavis And the music goes . . . (*she chants to the rhythm*) . . . da da da dada
da for nothing . . . da da da dada da back line . . . da da da dada da middle
line . . . da da da dada da Geoffrey . . .

They have attempted to turn, cross-legged, on the right beat

Sway, sway, arm up, hat down . . . and let's get into this big tap routine
you've all been waiting for! Right—it'll be easier with the music . . . and
here we go and . . .

*She repeats the same chant—and they try out the steps, clumsily, still having
much trouble crossing the legs*

OK, back into your opening positions and we'll try it again. Quick as you
can, please Rose, we've got a lot to get through . . . Dorothy—just a little
smaller . . . Sylvia, can we get rid of the gum? I want to see your teeth, not
hear them.

*As Sylvia takes the chewing gum from her mouth, Vera scuttles across to hold
out an ashtray to take the gum*

Vera! All right? And it's five six seven eight . . . Da da da dada da for
nothing . . . Da da da dada da back line . . . Da da da dada da middle line
. . . Sway sway Geoffrey!

Again their attempts have been clumsy

It's not working, is it, it's not clean enough, it looks tacky. OK, I think the
problem is that when you turn, some of you are a little off balance—so
let's try it so that instead of crossing your legs—watch—you step, put
both heels down and you're nice and solid.

They react appreciatively to this idea

Right, back into position please and we'll do it again—other way round
please Sylvia—and it's five six seven eight . . .

*They repeat the step, with Mrs Fraser playing the simple tune . . . and they are
chanting out the moves . . . and this time it works well and they beam with
pleasure*

That's much better—if feels better, yes?

They ad lib their happy agreement

OK, let's move on . . . it's all stuff you know—watch, and I'll talk you
through it . . . (*She chants, as she shows them the steps*) Fred As-taire, box
step box step, six tap springs bring you into one line . . . that's Maxine
Andy Vera Rose Geoffrey Sylvia Lynne and Dorothy.

Rose The two sore thumbs in the middle.

Mavis (*demonstrating*) Then . . . shuffle ball change, shuffle ball change shuffle ball change, six tap springs and hold. Right—let's try it to the music.

They protest that they aren't ready

Come on, come on, of course you can do it . . .

Before they can protest further—she indicates for Mrs Fraser to start playing

Five six seven eight . . .

They attempt the steps as she leads them, calling out the steps . . . and they get it hopelessly wrong, colliding into each other, shrieking their protests . . . and the Lights go quickly to Black-out and the sound of "Happy Feet" comes up and continues until the Lights come up for the next scene

SCENE 2

The same. Two weeks later

They are coming to the end of a session and are using bamboo canes and miming the use of hats. Their canework clearly leaves a lot to be desired, Andy dropping hers. Mavis kneels on the floor, consulting her notebook. And they come to the end of the section and Mrs Fraser stops playing ("Stepping Out")

Mavis Yes, that's not bad, not bad at all.
Andy (*hand up*) I'm still terribly worried about my stick.
Mavis What's the problem?
Andy I don't seem to have any control over it.
Mavis It'll come, don't worry, there's plenty of time. Sylvia—it's—(*she demonstrates*)—yes?
Sylvia The thing is . . . I know what it is in my head, I just can't get it through to my feet. (*She tries the step*)
Mavis Rose—you know what I'm going to say, don't you?
Rose (*peering from behind Geoffrey*) Stop hiding.
Mavis They want to see you.
Rose (*burying her head into Geoffrey*) Oh Jesus, don't remind me.
Mavis Think flash—if you've got it, flaunt it. Oh yes, Dorothy—you're still pushing too hard.
Dorothy Too hard—yes.
Mavis And the same goes for you, Andy—try and relax, nice and loose, yes?

Maxine is practising a step

Maxine—you don't seem very happy with the paddling and rolling.
Maxine (*still practising*) I'm delirious, darling, delirious.
Mavis Practise—OK?
Maxine I never stop, I'm obsessed—I'm even doing it in bed.
Lynne How can you do it in bed?
Maxine That's what *he* says.
Mavis Geoffrey—use your ankle— (*she demonstrates*)—pick up your toe

and bang it in, pick up your toe and bang it in. Lynne—what happened to
the time step?

Lynne I got carried away—sorry.

Mavis And you can't hold a stick and bite your nail at the same time—it
may taste good but it looks terrible. Oh yes—Rose—you're a step behind,
yes?

Rose is sitting in front of the stage, exhausted

Rose No angel, I'm forty years behind.

Mavis OK? Anything else? Well that's it for tonight, thank you very much
everyone, well done.

*Mrs Fraser instantly strikes up the piano roll as Mavis hurriedly collects her
things together and Vera collects the bamboo canes, like a school monitor
with:*

Vera Sticks to me!

All Sticks to Vera!

Mavis Can someone lock up for me tonight? I'm in rather a hurry.

Andy Yes, I can do it.

Mavis (*giving the key to Andy*) Just push it through his letterbox—thanks,
you're a love—and Andy, you're doing fine, everything's going to be all
right, I promise you.

Mavis (*suddenly remembering*) Oh yes—Maxine—(*she mimes*)—the hats.

Maxine Next week—definitely.

Mrs Fraser It was last week definitely.

Vera goes into the changing room

Rose picks up her bag and goes into the changing room

Sylvia and Maxine continue changing. Lynne and Dorothy have been talking

Lynne Isn't that awful, Geoffrey?

Geoffrey Sorry?

Dorothy I was just telling Lynne—it was so nice this lunch-time I thought
I'd go for a walk in the park—I like to go down by the lake and feed the
birds—you know—anyway, I was just feeding them and having such a
nice time when all of a sudden these two swans came swimming along,
you know the way they do, and before I knew it one of them was coming
out of the water, trying to attack me . . . hissing and spitting it was, I was
lucky to get away, it could have broken my leg, couldn't it, I was terrified.

Lynne They must have been jealous I suppose. I remember my dad was
always very worried about me feeding the swans.

Dorothy I mean, they're so beautiful, aren't they? Why do they have to be
so spiteful?

Geoffrey Did you know that when swans mate, they mate for life?

*Rose, now dressed, comes out of the changing room with her bag . . . and a
moment later Vera bustles out, wearing yellow rubber gloves and holding an
aerosol spray*

Vera Mavis . . .there is one thing we've been wondering . . . as it's a proper show and everything, will we be having Mrs Fraser or proper music?

Everyone waits for the reaction

Mrs Fraser I don't think I heard that.
Vera Not being funny or anything.
Mrs Fraser Who is this "we" might I ask?
Vera It was just a general topic of conversation. One or two of the girls.

Mrs Fraser eyes the "girls" beadily

Mrs Fraser I see.
Mavis (*stepping in quickly and clearly winging it*) I know what you mean, Vera, and the reason I haven't said anything definite yet is because I'm still waiting to hear something from Liz . . . it really depends on what facilities they have available—whether we have Glenda or Glenda with maybe a couple of other musicians . . . or whether we just use a tape—that sounds about right, doesn't it, Glenda, you've done quite a few of these shows.
Mrs Fraser In my experience . . . it depends entirely upon the standard. (*Her tone makes it quite clear what she thinks the standard to be*) I shall wait by the car.

She goes out, stone-faced

Mavis Yes, well, thank you Vera—you might have waited until I said something—good-night everyone—you won't forget the lights, will you Andy?

They ad lib their good-nights as

Mavis goes out

The others regard Vera in silence

Vera Well we need to know, don't we?

She bustles back into the changing room

Geoffrey goes behind the notice-board to change

Maxine Well she should be a good dancer, she certainly knows how to put her foot in it.
Lynne Well *I* didn't say anything.
Dorothy I certainly didn't, did I?
Rose Oh well, her heart's in the right place.
Sylvia You reckon?
Lynne I have been wondering though.
Maxine Of course we're going to have proper music—it's a show, we can't just have a piano.
Sylvia You wouldn't hear it with all us lot banging around.
Dorothy Yes, but she hasn't actually said, has she?
Maxine She's keeping the old duck happy—common sense.

She looks under a chair in front of the stage for the lighter she has lost as Lynne and Dorothy go towards the changing room with their bags

Lynne Did I hear her mention something about singing?
Andy Singing?
Lynne I think that's what she said, yes.

Dorothy and Lynne go off

Andy (*worried*) I didn't know about singing ... does anyone know about singing?

Vera bustles out of the changing room, still in the gloves and with the aerosol

Behind the notice-board, Geoffrey is changing

Vera These windows are filthy—(*She realizes Geoffrey is taking his trousers down and turns away sharply*) Sorry Geoffrey.

Below the notice board, we see Geoffrey's tracksuit trousers drop down around his ankles, exposing his bare legs. Maxine, still looking for her lighter, sees this—grins—gesticulates to the others—and pretends to try and see up Geoffrey's legs

Maxine I say—Geoffrey ...

Geoffrey's head appears above the board

Are those your own legs?

She moves away, grinning, and Geoffrey hastily sets about dressing himself

Vera These windows are filthy.
Sylvia I'll send my Terry round.
Vera Is he a window cleaner?
Sylvia Now and again.
Vera Only I thought you said he was a scaffolder.
Sylvia That was previous.
Maxine Previous to what?
Sylvia Previous to getting the Big E.
Vera Pardon?
Sylvia (*miming*) Elbow.
Vera Oh you mean like tennis elbow.
Sylvia No I mean like getting layed off.
Maxine All I ever see nowadays is men with a bucket and ladder.
Sylvia That's your moonlighting, innit?
Vera Lionel's been with his company for twenty-seven years.
Sylvia Be retiring soon then, will he?
Vera Oh, he'll never retire, not Lionel.
Maxine I think you'll find he might have to.
Vera What I mean is, he's one of these men who loves working.
Maxine Well when he does retire, perhaps he can hold the ladder for her Terry.
Vera Oh, he'd never do anything manual, he works with his brain.

Sylvia Here—you live in Leicester Road, don't you Maxine?
Maxine Number sixty-eight—why?
Sylvia My Terry does Leicester Road.
Maxine My bloke's called John.
Sylvia That's him, John.
Vera You said his name was Terry.
Sylvia It is. John's his working name. (*To Maxine*) Not a bad-looker, is he—done the insides for you yet, has he?
Vera How d'you mean, his working name?

Dorothy, now dressed and carrying her bicycle basket etc., comes out of the changing room and moves across to look at the notice-board, waiting for Lynne

Rose She means he's on the dole.
Vera (*not understanding*) Oh yes?
Sylvia He has to keep the old diamond polishing on the q.t. so he calls himself John just in case.
Vera Just in case what?
Maxine Do you live in this world, Vera?
Geoffrey In case someone informs on him.

They turn to regard him for a moment

Sylvia There's some very dodgy people about. (*She leans into Vera*) Snoopers.
Geoffrey (*unable to resist*) You mean he's drawing unemployment and earning money at the same time.
Sylvia Don't get snotty, Geoffrey, they're all at it—right?

Lynne comes out of the changing room with her bag. She moves straight across to Dorothy and they exit, calling out their good-nights

Vera goes towards the changing room, pausing at Geoffrey with

Vera (*confidentially*) I don't think that's very nice, do you, Geoffrey?

She continues into the changing room

Andy is changing her shoes

Sylvia You're definitely not coming for a drink then.
Rose We're only having the one quickie.
Maxine No, no, I'd better get back—I promised Wonderboy I'd help him find his mascara.
Sylvia I wonder if that Simon will be there?
Maxine Who's Simon?
Sylvia This amazingly dubious person we met down the wine bar last week.
Rose You've got to stop talking to these people.
Sylvia Stone me, Rose, you aren't half mournful at times.
Rose They get the wrong idea and then you got trouble.
Andy (*suddenly*) Doesn't your husband mind?

They look at her

I'm sorry, I'm fascinated, that's all.
Sylvia What—you mean me having a night out?
Andy Well, yes, I mean . . .
Sylvia Thursday's my night out, innit? He babysits, I go out.
Rose He'd mind if he thought you were talking to the likes of Simple Simon.
Sylvia He knows, don'ee?
Andy You mean you . . . you mean you—talk to him about it?
Sylvia No, I don't talk to him about it, do I, I tell him.

Andy mouths the word "Oh" . . . nodding slightly, not realizing she's being sent up

Leave it out, Andy, he loves it. That's why I do it. If he believed me he'd kill me—what he enjoys is the idea of being jealous—and it does wonders for your sex life which let's face it and close your ears, Geoffrey, takes a severe bashing after the first few months of hanging from the chandelier. We used to do it more before we were married—well you do, don't you?

Andy looks as though she's never done it at any time and certainly not lately

Maxine (*joining in on the sending up of Andy*) Friend of mine was married ten years and every day he wants sex. Not once—three times. Three times a day for ten years. In the end she had to divorce him. Over-consummation of marital rights.
Rose I'm not surprised, the man is sick. Where's he living now?
Sylvia Come on, Rosie, good-night all, see you next week. (*She picks up her bag*)
Maxine Good-night girls.

Sylvia and Rose go quickly towards the door

Rose—remind your Paul it's quarter to eight sharp in the morning.
Rose He already told me.
Sylvia How's he doing, your Paul?
Rose He's OK, she's very pleased with him.

Sylvia and Rose go out

Maxine turns to take up her bag. A little look passes between Andy and Geoffrey

But then Vera is coming out of the changing room with

Vera Oh you are still here, Geoffrey—good—I wonder if you'd mind giving me a hand with the cupboard.
Geoffrey (*moving towards her*) Yes of course, what's the, umm . . .
Vera I want to put my cleaning things away and the door's jammed. (*As they go inside*) Thanks ever so much, they're awful those sea scouts, aren't they—sorry to be a nuisance.

Maxine stands for a moment, looking at Andy. Andy starts straightening the chairs

Maxine Good-night Andy.
Andy (*stiffly*) Good-night.

A moment

Maxine We seem to rub each other up the wrong way, don't we?
Andy I really haven't thought about it.
Maxine I think so.
Andy We are what we are. (*With a flat smile*) Isn't that what they say?

She pushes a chair into place as Maxine looks at her for a moment

Maxine I used to do all this dancing stuff at school. If you think I'm full of
shit now you should have seen me then—the Tiller girls had nothing on
me, I was terrific. Life was terrific—all spread out, just waiting for me to
take advantage. Twenty years later, twenty years of deflection and getting
most of it wrong and I suddenly realize that the one thing I don't have any
more is confidence. Big family joke: Maxine The Mouth is totally lacking
in self-confidence. Coming to these classes is not so much self-indulgence
as doctor's orders. It's therapy. And it works and now I go home less tired
than when I came. Able to cope. Resenting it if anything gets in the way of
my coming here. So what am I saying? So what I'm saying is, maybe what
we are, you and me, isn't all that much different.

Geoffrey comes out of the changing room

Good-night Geoffrey.

Maxine goes out

Geoffrey pulls on his raincoat and we see that he has a bandage on his finger

Geoffrey How long d'you think before we, um . . .?
Andy I didn't come by car tonight, I'm afraid.
Geoffrey Oh. I see.
Andy My husband's collecting me at quarter past. He couldn't make it any
earlier, that's why I offered to . . .

She vaguely indiates "tidy up". He nods

Vera comes out of the changing room with her bag

Vera It's terrible when you have to lock things up, isn't it? Sorry about your
finger, Geoffrey—lucky I had my little box, wasn't it? Are we off then?
Andy I'm waiting for my husband actually.
Vera Oh, I'll wait with you then, shall I?
Andy Geoffrey's already offered.
Geoffrey Oh—yes.
Vera I don't mind, Geoffrey—really.
Geoffrey Well if you're sure—I mean . . .
Vera I'm not in any hurry tonight—really—go on, Geoffrey, off you go.
Geoffrey Well I do have things to do . . . (*He looks at Andy*)

Andy can scarcely conceal her disappointment

I'll see you next week then. Good-night.
Vera } *(together)* { Good-night Geoffrey.
Andy }   { Good-night.

A moment's hesitation and he takes up his briefcase and goes out

Andy There's really no need for either of you to stay.
Vera It's only a few minutes, isn't it?

Andy moves to close the piano lid and then sits at the piano

To be quite honest, my two are both out. They're at the Festival Hall—some sort of concert—and they're bound to have a little bite afterwards, they usually do. I think it's nice for a father and daughter to go out together, don't you? Your son's at boarding school, isn't he, Andy?
Andy Yes.
Vera Still. Holidays soon. I expect you'll be glad to have him home. You'd think they'd tidy this up a bit, wouldn't you? By the way, I'm thinking of making some curtains for the changing-room window—I can cut them down from an old pair—I never throw anything away, you know, I drive poor Lionel mad—I think he'd leave me if I didn't have my own work-room—only joking, we're ever so happy, we really are—not that I'm a prude or anything but anyone can see into that window, can't they? I'll just check the size, actually—(*she indicates her bag*)—I've got my tape, well you never know, do you?

She goes through into the changing room

A moment. Andy looks at the piano, then raises the lid, looks at the keyboard, and then, with one finger, pecks out the first three notes of "Stepping Out". As she does, we hear the bip-bip of a car horn outside. She stops playing momentarily ... then begins again ... then begins striking the notes with her clenched fist ...

Vera is looking at her through the changing-room door

Andy bangs away violently, tunelessly as——

The Lights fade to Black-out and the sound of "Happy Feet" comes up. The music continue and then fades as the Lights come up for the next scene

SCENE 3

The same. Two weeks later, June

Andy, Sylvia and Lynne are in a group, practising with their bamboo canes. The bottom twelve inches or so of Sylvia's cane is covered in white paint. Geoffrey is replacing the plug on a small electric fan, using his Swiss penknife, and watched by an interfering Vera. Dorothy sits, blowing her nose. She has hay fever and has a box of tissues under the chair with her bag. Mavis, in her tracksuit, is trying—and failing—to open a window. She is edgy and bad-tempered. She gives up and moves to her chair to light a cigarette

Maxine enters, carrying her cane, bag with shoes and a large cardboard box tied with string

Maxine (*generally*) Sorry. (*She puts down the box and quickly changes into her tap shoes*)
Vera Thankseversomuch Geoffrey. (*She takes the fan from him and looks around*) Where d'you think I should put it?
Sylvia Vera wants to know where she should put her fan.
Vera Where d'you think, Mavis?
Mavis (*indicating*) There's a plug over there, isn't there?

Vera plugs the fan in near the stage

Mrs Fraser comes out of the changing room and moves to the piano. She sits, opening her magazine

Mrs Fraser Are we starting or what?
Mavis (*generally*) Did she say anything to anyone? Sylvia?
Sylvia I haven't seen her.
Mavis It doesn't look like she's coming then, does it?
Maxine What's happened?
Lynne Rose isn't here.
Vera It doesn't work.
Sylvia Vera's fan doesn't work.
Geoffrey The wires are all right.
Mavis (*indicating*) There's one here, try it here.

Vera tries the fan in the socket near the piano as Dorothy sneezes

Lynne Bless you.
Dorothy Excuse me. (*She blows violently into a tissue*)
Mavis OK—we'll have to assume she's not coming.
Sylvia I don't understand it.

Vera switches on the fan and it begins to work, rather noisily

Vera There.
Sylvia What would we do without you, Vera?
Mavis (*putting her cigarette into the ashtray*) Those are the hats, are they Maxine? Can we have them, please?
Mrs Fraser Oh, the famous hats have finally put in an appearance, have they?

Geoffrey moves to untie the box string with his penknife, but Maxine waves him away. Mrs Fraser pointedly moves the ashtray further away and Sylvia cools her behind over the fan

Mavis What we'll do is concentrate on the bits where the hats are important.
Geoffrey Won't Rose not being here, umm . . .
Mavis We can't worry about Rose, there isn't time, she can pick it up later. But please—if any of you can't make the class—say so. We'll take it from the section where you take the hats off.

Mrs Fraser Excuse me.

Mavis Yes Glenda.

Mrs Fraser Will you be requiring some form of introduction or shall I make do with a starting pistol?

Maxine Ta-ra! (*She triumphantly holds up a hat, but her face drops instantly*)

Dorothy That's not a straw hat.

Maxine Get away.

Andy I thought you were bringing the boaters.

Maxine So did I. Look what he's given me. (*She produces another hat—a trilby*)

Andy Didn't you check them?

Maxine I ask for straw hats, I expect the man to give me straw hats.

Dorothy You should have checked though, Maxine.

Maxine Should? What's this word "should"?

Geoffrey (*taking out a boater*) Here's one.

Sylvia Geoffrey's found a boater.

Dorothy Well that's something, isn't it?

Andy They'll be all right to practise with, won't they?

Mavis (*sighing heavily*) Not really—no—they won't.

Maxine Next week—I guarantee.

Mrs Fraser (*reading*) Would someone kindly give that needle a shove.

Maxine (*generally*) I'm sorry—I'm very sorry.

Geoffrey Umm . . . could we not use them anyway, um, Mavis . . . at least we'll have the feel of actually, er . . .

He mimes removing a hat and the others ad lib their agreement. Mavis is on the point of screaming, but—with an effort at calm

Mavis OK everyone, grab a hat and we'll go through it—quickly please.

They move in like vultures to grab a hat—Geoffrey managing to keep hold of his boater. Mavis draws a deep breath on her cigarette. She becomes aware of Mrs Fraser regarding her smugly

Don't say it—I'm not in the mood.

Mrs Fraser purses her lips and slowly shakes her head in disdain at the proceedings. They've all grabbed a hat except Dorothy

Dorothy There's one missing.

Maxine I don't believe it.

Sylvia Look on the bright side—if Rose had been here there would have been two missing.

Mavis sits, controlling her anger

Maxine I ask for eight, I get six.

Mrs Fraser Perhaps it's by way of your usual discount.

Vera, Andy, Lynne and Sylvia are more concerned with looking at themselves in the mirror

Dorothy I haven't got a hat, Mavis.

Mavis You'll just have to mime it.
Dorothy I've been miming it all month.
Mavis Then you should be very good at it.
Andy You can have mine.
Dorothy No, it's all right—really.
Lynne We can swap later on.
Dorothy No, it's all right—I don't mind—really. (*She sneezes violently into her tissue*)
Andy ⎫ (*together*) ⎰ Bless you.
Lynne ⎭
Mavis OK everyone, let's have you on the diagonal—you know your positions—quickly please—you'll need your stick, Sylvia ...

Sylvia grabs her stick and hurries back into line

Can I have a straight line, please—no a *straight* line on the diagonal, it's not that difficult, surely? Do your army thing, will you Geoffrey, or we'll be here all night.

Geoffrey stands vaguely to attention, thrusting out his arm, army-style, and the others measure off from him, larking around

No, you haven't left a gap for Rose—try and think what you're doing, it does help.

The line widens as they shuffle out, leaving a gap for Rose ... and Geoffrey crashes into Mrs Fraser at the piano, causing her to play an involuntary chord ... which makes the class even more giggly

Geoffrey My fault, sorry.
Mavis And for chrissake stop biting your nail, Lynne.
Lynne Sorry.
Mavis Is anyone feeling hot?

General murmurings of "Not really ... Not yet" etc.

Right—can we have that thing off for the minute, Vera, I can't hear myself think.

Vera, rather like a chastened child, moves to switch off the fan

Maxine (*to Sylvia, of her painted stick*) What's that for?
Sylvia He only used it to stir a tin of paint, didn't he? I've been helped across the road three times.
Mavis OK, so it's five six seven eight ...

Mrs Fraser plays and they clumsily go through the steps

No, you still haven't got the movement right ... (*She takes one of their hats and demonstrates as*) Now please—watch—one and two, arms straight ... (*She returns the hat*) Do it again—five six seven eight ...

They do it again ... without much more success ... and Dorothy sneezes and Andy drops her hat causing minor chaos down the line. Mrs Fraser stops playing

They wait for Mavis' pronouncement

Mavis Look—I think I've made a mistake. It's too complicated.

Andy I really am terribly sorry.

Mavis No it isn't just you, Andy—it's everyone—having both the hat and the stick is giving you too much to think about—it's too complicated, I don't think it's going to work.

Maxine Oh. (*She does a bit with her hat and stick, making it clear that she personally can cope*)

Andy (*hand up*) Can I say something?

Mavis Yes Andy.

Andy To be quite honest—well I know I'm not exactly an expert on these——

Mavis What do you want to say, Andy?

Andy Well ... to be honest ... I could never quite understand why we were having them at all.

Dorothy Having what?

Lynne The hat and the stick.

Dorothy Oh.

Sylvia It's obvious, innit? It's to draw attention away from our feet—right, Mavis?

Maxine Speak for yourself, darling.

Lynne I thought it was because—well, they all have them, don't they? It's all part of the image.

Dorothy Image—yes.

Maxine Razzle dazzle—I love it.

Lynne I mean, they nearly always have a hat and a stick, don't they?

Maxine (*singing, dancing*) "Give 'em the old razzle dazzle, razzle dazzle 'em ..."

Mavis (*firmly*) It isn't working—my fault, but it isn't working, it's tacky. I think it should be one or the other.

Vera Oh God.

Sylvia It's not that bad.

Vera No, I've snared my tights.

Mavis I think we should lose the sticks.

Dorothy Sticks—yes.

Maxine It's a bit late in the day, Mavis.

Andy I thought I was quite good with the stick.

Dorothy I've been practising with mine ever such a lot.

Lynne Yes, I have.

Sylvia So have I. When I could find it.

Andy What I mean is ... I've learned it all.

All this has come quickly

Mavis Yes I know you don't like things being altered, Andy, but you'll have to start getting used to it—I'll be changing things all the time, that's ... (*she trails off*). Look. When you use sticks, it's got to be neat and precise and absolutely on the button. You haven't got it yet and with the time we've got left, I don't think you ever will. I know you're trying, it's not your fault, it's my fault, I put them in and now I'm taking them out—so let's get rid of the sticks and run through the final part with just the hats.

She turns away as Vera collects up the sticks

Vera Sticks to me!
All Sticks to Vera!
Mrs Fraser I warned you you'd bitten off more than they can chew.
Mavis Let's take it from the first Fred Astaire without the sticks ... and it's five six seven eight ...

They run through the same section, using just the hats—Dorothy sneezing just when she should be doing her bit and getting out of sync. They stop

Andy It feels strange without the stick.
Vera It does feel ever so awkward now, I must say.
Dorothy Say—yes.
Andy It's with the arm doing nothing.
Vera It's as though you need something to get hold of.
Dorothy Hold of—yes.
Sylvia Geoffrey—I think the time has come for you to make the supreme sacrifice.
Geoffrey Sorry?
Andy Why do you have to reduce everything to ... (*She trails off*)
Sylvia To what?
Andy It doesn't matter.
Sylvia Apparently it does matter.
Mavis (*clapping her hands*) All right all right ... by this time next week you'll have forgotten all about the sticks, I promise you.
Mrs Fraser Oh yes?
Mavis OK, we'll go through the middle section. There's really no point in going on until we've got the proper hats.
Maxine (*generally*) I'm very sorry.
Lynne Shall we keep the hats on or what?
Mavis I don't care, I really don't care—I just want to see you go through your individual bits with Geoffrey. (*She has said this with mounting anger and frustration. Then she moves to Mrs Fraser, indicating which section she's talking about*)
Sylvia I was just pulling your leg, that's all Geoffrey.
Geoffrey I think we're all a little bit—you know.
Sylvia You're the only fellah, I'm bound to pull your leg, right?
Andy (*moving to them*) I'm sorry, I shouldn't have ...
Sylvia Forget it.
Andy Yes, but I really shouldn't have ...
Sylvia Listen—we're all a bit uptight what with four weeks to go and madam being so umpty—forget it.

Maxine—whose hat is a bowler—does some simple but effective trick stuff with it as Mavis moves away from Mrs Fraser, clapping her hands

Mav   o ... Geoffrrey is downstage right and the rest of you in a big
V

Dorothy sneezes, dropping her hat

Andy ⎫
Lynne ⎬ (*together*) ⎰ Bless you.
Vera ⎭
Maxine (*at the same time*) *Gesundheit.*
Mavis Isn't there anything you can do about that, Dorothy?
Dorothy I'm sorry, it's the pollen.
Mavis OK, OK ... Geoffrey downstage right and the rest of you——

Dorothy blows her nose loudly

— the rest of you in a big V. You'll have to mime the bit with Rose,
Geoffrey ... no, on second thoughts, I'll stand in for her ... you're all
marking time ... (*she demonstrates as*) ... Geoffrey turns you one by one
... you touch hands ... and tap springs ... like this ... one two three four
five six seven and reverse two three four five six seven and reverse two
three four five six seven ...

She guides Geoffrey in the movement until he gets where Rose should be

Thank you, Geoffrey ... once more then and this time you mime it with
Rose, OK Geoffrey and here we go and ...

*They repeat the steps, this time with Mrs Fraser playing simple piano vamps
and the class calling out the steps "... two three four five six seven and reverse
two three four five six seven ..." etc. When Geoffrey forgets to mime the
movement for Rose, they chime "Mime, mime" ... and so on down the line
until he comes to Dorothy at the end and she gets into a tangle so that he is not
so much turning her as wrestling with her ... so that once again, it ends in
chaos, with them laughing and nudging each other and Mavis looking on
angrily ... and then*

Lynne Can I say something, Mavis?
Mavis Yes, Lynne.
Lynne I've been thinking, you see, Mavis—and I was wondering if—when
we do this bit—we might all do something different. I know it's very
important that we're a team and everything but I just thought this might
be the one moment where we could all do something—well—individual.

Vague rumblings of agreement from some of the others

Mavis I see.
Lynne What I really meant, Mavis ... was that as Geoffrey's the only man
and the rest of us are, you know—whether we couldn't all have a different
relationship with him. Only in this section, I mean.
Mavis (*flat*) What do you mean, Lynne, a different relationship?
Lynne Well ... sort of like ... he's the one man and we're the sort of
different women in his life and the sort of things we do could show the sort
of different relationships. Sort of.

Dorothy Oh I see what you mean—yes.

Mavis (*sarcastically*) You mean don't just move it, motivate it.

Dorothy Motivate it—yes.

Lynne (*already losing faith in the idea*) It's just sort of an idea I had.

Mavis All right, give me an example.

Lynne Well I don't——

Mavis You say you've thought about it—all right—give me an example.

Lynne Well ... I could be his daughter and he could be sort of giving me away.

Sylvia I could be his wife and he could be sort of ignoring me.

Mavis Dorothy could be his next-door neighbour and he could be sort of borrowing a pint of milk.

Lynne It was only an idea.

Maxine I know what Lynne means though Mavis because I've been thinking the same thing myself.

Mavis Oh yes?

Maxine As a matter of fact I'd worked a little something out—d'you mind if I show you?

Mavis Go ahead.

Maxine What I was thinking was ...

She takes the unwilling Geoffrey, guides him to the centre, gets him down on one knee and, holding his hand, does some turns around him, as

He's on his knee ... he turns me this way ... he turns me this way ... and I end up, on his knee, facing out front.

She holds her pose on Geoffrey's knee, beaming out front, then looks to Mavis for approval

It's only a suggestion.

Mavis Has anyone else got any suggestions?

Suddenly all the others—apart from Geoffrey and Andy—are chipping in, as they turn to each other in pairs to try out ideas that have taken their fancy ... "If I did this, Geoffrey could ..." "... I think it would be nice if ..." etc. and suddenly

Shut up! All of you, shut up!

They stop, stunned by her outburst

You've each got two bars solo with Geoffrey ... get him on your own and work out what you want to do with him ... bearing in mind what you can do, not what you think you can do which believe me is something quite different. You've got five minutes.

Snatching up her cigarettes, she goes into the changing room

A moment

Mrs Fraser I hope you're all very pleased with yourselves.

And, not without satisfaction, she gets up and goes out after Mavis

Lynne It was only a suggestion.
Dorothy She's in a really bad mood, isn't she.
Vera It's not like Mavis, she's been picking on us all night.
Sylvia Well let's face it, we have been mucking about a bit.
Maxine It was the hats.
Lynne No, she was like it before you came.
Dorothy Came—yes. Look at Vera's fan.
Vera I was only trying to be helpful.

Dorothy sneezes

Sylvia That doesn't help either.
Dorothy I can't help it, it's the pollen.
Andy And what with Rose not being here, I suppose.
Vera She should have said something, you know.
Sylvia What are you looking at me for?
Geoffrey I think she's probably worried in case we—let her down.
Dorothy Down—yes.
Geoffrey I mean . . . whatever we do reflects on her teaching ability really, doesn't it?
Lynne I thought it would be a good idea, that's all. I didn't mean to interfere or anything.
Andy Well what do you suggest we do? We can't just stand here.
Maxine Right—who's going to start?
Sylvia Start what?
Maxine Doing something with Geoffrey.
Sylvia Who wants to do something with Geoffrey?

Vague murmurings of indecision

Andy Oh look—I'll go first, I don't mind.
Sylvia Go on, Andy, get in there.
Andy Well someone's got to start, haven't they? Geoffrey?
Geoffrey Umm . . . yes . . . what did you, er . . .

They move away to talk and try out little steps, working it up together, as the others split into groups. Dorothy and Lynne work together, Dorothy taking the man's part as

Vera It's not like Mavis though, is it?
Maxine Maybe she's just had a bad day.
Vera I expect it's the curse, I know I get ever so ratty.
Sylvia Probably had a row with the old man.
Vera I don't think they're married actually—I think they live together.
Sylvia How shocking.
Vera And reading between the lines, I think she has rather a bad time with him. (*Confidentially*) Money. Have you noticed her shoes? Always wears the same shoes.

Maxine She can't make much out of this, that's for sure—not once she's paid for the Hall.

Vera And Mrs Fraser.

Maxine Even seven nights a week she's not going to make a fortune.

Vera No, I'm just saying, reading between the lines, he's not much of a provider.

Sylvia Reading between what lines?

Vera Have you never heard the way Mrs Fraser goes on about him?

Sylvia She says a lot about a lot of things—beats me why Mavis puts up with it.

Vera Well she's really like a sort of second mother, isn't she?

Sylvia Who is?

Vera Mrs Fraser—to Mavis.

Sylvia I dunno.

Vera Oh yes. (*Confidentially*) As I understand it, Mavis' mother walked out on them when she was, oh, tiny—Mavis I mean—and Mrs Fraser, who was living next door at the time——

Sylvia How do you find out all these things, Vera?

Vera People talk to me. I suppose it's because I'm such a sympathetic listener.

But Maxine is nudging them with

Maxine Hello—look at Ginger Rogers.

They turn to regard Andy and Geoffrey who are trying to do a step, rather clumsily, Andy's back arched as he bends her backwards

I wonder what sort of relationship she's got in mind.

Andy moves away from Geoffrey self-consciously

Lynne Can I try something with you, Geoffrey?

Sylvia Come on, Dotty, let's have a go ...

So that they are trying steps as

Mavis enters, followed a moment later by Mrs Fraser

They stop dancing and wait as Mavis moves to the front, tossing down her cigarettes and Mrs Fraser moves to sit at the piano, not looking at anyone

Mavis Well?

A moment

Lynne Not very good, actually.

Mavis OK. You can't do it for yourselves, you've got to accept the fact that I tell you what to do—yes?

Lynne I wasn't trying to——

Mavis It's probably a good idea that each of you does something different. I'll bring something in next week and you can work on it individually with Geoffrey.

We get their pleased if somewhat surprised reactions as

And if I can say this just once . . . I lost my temper, I shouldn't have and it won't happen again. Now if we can get on——
Vera No, it was our fault, Mavis, and we're very sorry.
Mavis Yes, all right Vera, thank you.

They are all speaking at the same time again as

Sylvia We were messing you about.
Maxine What with the hats being all wrong.
Andy Rose not being here.
Dorothy Being here.
Geoffrey And not being able to do the, um, sticks.
Andy We know it's important to you.
Sylvia We just got a bit silly.
Lynne I think we're all a bit nervous, really.
Dorothy Nervous—yes.
Andy You were bound to get upset.
Vera We do understand, Mavis—really.

It has all come quickly and already Mavis' nerves are jangling again . . . so that she puts her hands over her ears

Mavis No you don't understand! I'm bloodywell pregnant and I don't want to be—can you understand *that*?

This moment. They are stunned into silence. Even Mrs Fraser has reacted. Mavis remains with her hands to her head for a moment and then

OK. Let's take it right back from the top . . . you know your positions.

They obediently move into their opening positions . . . in the two lines with Geoffrey at the front, their backs to us

When you're ready, Glenda. And it's five six seven eight . . .

They begin their dancing . . . the back line, middle line and then Geoffrey turning to the front. The tempo of the piano playing, and the way they dance, reflect the stunned mood of the moment. So that they turn and go into their opening steps like lifeless puppets, no expression on their faces . . . and they continue dancing like this for a moment
The Lights fade slowly to Black-out and the sound of "Happy Feet" comes up and continues until the Lights come up for the next scene

SCENE 4

The same. Three weeks later. June

Mavis is at the notice-board, putting up a poster for the show. Andy sits tying on her tap shoes which have been dyed black. She has a bandage around her hand and wrist. She will be even more edgy than usual tonight. Maxine has brought a pile of striped blazers and fishnet stockings. She distributes the stockings as Vera kneels, pinning up Sylvia's blazer. Sylvia seems unusually disinterested in the proceedings . . . as Lynne and Rose decide to exchange their blazers to see if they fit better . . . as Geoffrey takes up his boater and puts it on to look at the general effect in the mirror and is not displeased . . . All this as

Maxine (*to Geoffrey*) And a buttonhole, I think you should have a nice buttonhole.
Lynne (*of Rose's blazer*) Oh that's much better.
Rose There's not much room for negotiation.
Lynne They won't be buttoned up anyway—how does mine look?
Vera Mavis.
Mavis Yes, Vera.
Maxine A carnation maybe, to match the tie.
Vera I was wondering about length.
Mavis Not with you.
Vera Well I was thinking . . . could you stand in a line please girls—and Geoffrey, sorry Geoffrey—(*she ushers them into a rough line as*)—what I could do is try and make them all the same length—so that the bottoms all line up—are you with me?
Sylvia What bottoms?
Vera Look, I'll show you.

She moves along the line, getting each of them to hold their blazer where she folds it up at the bottom as:

Dorothy hurries in with her bicycle basket

Dorothy Sorry.

She hurries into the changing room

Vera stands back and indicates the blazers

Vera What d'you think?
Mavis It's a nice idea but I don't think so.
Vera It would look ever so effective.
Rose It would look a lot more effective if *our* bottoms all lined up.
Vera But that's what it would look like, you see.
Sylvia Are you kidding?
Mavis Yes it's a nice idea but I don't think so, Vera, really. Now what was I going to say—oh yes—shoes. I think it might be a good idea if you all had loose taps fitted.
Lynne Like the professionals use.
Mavis Right—the difference is amazing, I promise you—you'll really know you're tapping.
Geoffrey Can we get them locally?
Vera That shop in Northfields Lane is very good actually.
Rose I wouldn't go to that woman's shop if she had the last pair of tap shoes on earth, that is an awful person.

Sylvia Why can't we just loosen the ones we've got? (*She lifts a foot to regard the sole of her shoe, toppling against the others*)

Mrs Fraser comes out of the changing room, straightening her hat

Mavis I tell you what, if you'd all like to give me your shoes when we've finished tonight, I'll go to Freed's, buy some taps and get them put on for next week—OK?

General murmurs of agreement

Mrs Fraser (*sitting at the piano*) More running about. (*She takes up her magazine to read*)

Dorothy hurries out of the changing room with her handbag

Maxine Dorothy.

She holds up a blazer. Dorothy tries on the blazer, looking at herself in the mirror, as

Dorothy Isn't it exciting?
Sylvia (*quietly*) I'd like a word with you, Dorothy.
Dorothy Sorry?
Mavis Has everyone ordered their tickets?

General indications of yes and no

Well they're going pretty fast apparently so anyone who hasn't, can you do it now, please?

Dorothy and Rose move to Mrs Fraser who notes their ticket order as

Lynne Do we know about the hall yet, Mavis?
Mavis Oh—yes—thanks Lynne—(*generally*)—the only time we can have the hall for extra rehearsal next week is on Tuesday.
Mrs Fraser (*to Dorothy*) How many?
Dorothy Nine.
Mrs Fraser Oh yes—coach party, is it?
Dorothy My colleagues from the office. They're really looking forward to it.
Mrs Fraser I can imagine.
Mavis How does that suit everyone?

Everyone makes noises of agreement. Andy has hastily consulted her diary

Dorothy (*to Rose*) I shall have to get a sitter but I'm sure it will be all right.
Rose For your mother, is it?
Dorothy Mother—yes.
Rose If you want, I'll ask my daughter.
Dorothy Oh I'm sure I'll manage, thank you Rose.
Andy Oh dear. That's the nineteenth.
Dorothy She's a bit funny, my mother. You know—a bit old-fashioned.
Mavis What's the problem?
Andy I've got a meeting on the nineteenth. No, no, it's all right, I can cancel.

Maxine (*to Lynne*) Always a drama.
Lynne (*to Maxine, quietly*) You shouldn't say that, she can't help it, can she, she's——
Mavis We're all OK then, are we? Lynne?
Lynne Yes, I'm getting someone to stand in for me.
Vera (*pinning Sylvia's sleeve*) Can you keep still a seccy, Sylvia?
Geoffrey So that's just two more rehearsals.
Rose (*holding her stomach*) Don't say it.
Mavis And the dress on the twenty-second.
Dorothy That's in the big hall, is it, Mavis?
Mavis That's in the big hall.
Rose Oh Jesus—just thinking about it turns my stomach over.
Dorothy I know—isn't it exciting?
Sylvia Can I move now or what?
Vera Yes all done thankseversomuch Sylvia.

Sylvia takes off her blazer and gives it to Vera as

Mavis And don't forget—it's full costume, full make-up, the lot.
Vera I must remember to get my hair done.
Dorothy I don't think I shall have time.
Maxine Borrow Rose's wig.
Rose Sure—if the cat's finished with it.
Vera (*to Maxine*) Sylvia's very quiet tonight, don't you think, Maxine?
Mavis (*of the blazers*) When d'you think they might be ready, Vera?

Up on the stage, Mavis talks to Vera about the blazers as Maxine and Rose talk together about the fishnets as Lynne takes up her Sony Walkman, puts on the headphones and a boater and practises quietly on her own—and then Dorothy joins her and Lynne lets her listen in on the headphones as Andy moves to Geoffrey who has taken a sheet of paper from his suit pocket and is sitting, reading it. Sylvia was going to speak to Dorothy, but seeing her go to Lynne, she instead joins Maxine and Rose as

Andy You haven't ordered any tickets.
Geoffrey No—there isn't really anyone I, um . . . (*He smiles*) Not that I'm sorry.
Andy Most of my friends are coming whether I want them to or not.
Geoffrey (*smiling*) Yes.
Andy God knows what they expect. Or want to expect. Anyway. They'll have something new to talk about, won't they?
Maxine Why don't I suggest it?
Sylvia No odds to me, one way or the other.
Rose Why you so miserable about everything?

Maxine moves to speak to Mavis and Vera, so that these three are up on the stage, as

Sylvia Mind your own.

Rose Don't take it out on me, girl—we all got the jitters.
Mavis I hadn't really thought about it.
Vera It would be nice though.
Mavis (*generally*) What does everyone feel about having a little party afterwards?
Vera Just a few bottles of wine and some dips or something.
Maxine What d'you think?

They generally confer as

Mrs Fraser I know what I think.
Andy (*to Geoffrey*) I can't imagine anything worse.
Vera I could do my taramasalata.
Lynne Where would we have it?
Maxine At my place—yeah, why not?
Rose You mean just us.
Maxine No—bring who you like.
Dorothy You mean a proper party.
Maxine Why not? I'll get Wonderboy to do a barbecue.
Lynne That sounds lovely.
Dorothy Lovely—yes. If it doesn't rain.
Maxine So he'll get wet.
Vera I could do my kebabs.
Maxine With his personality, who'll notice?

They generally confer as

Andy (*taking the plunge*) My husband won't be here that weekend, he's away with my son. I thought we might possibly ... I mean, rather than a party, I thought you might like ... well, a meal or something. (*And already she's embarrassed at her forwardness and*) ... only if you'd like to, of course, I'm not trying to ...
Maxine That's agreed then, is it? Andy?
Andy Well I'm not sure actually—I did vaguely promise someone that I'd um ...

She is looking to Geoffrey who avoids her eyes

Maxine Suit yourself—Geoffrey?
Geoffrey I think it sounds a very good idea, um, Maxine—yes—thank you.
Mavis OK everyone, let's get on shall we or we'll have nothing to celebrate.

She sits to put on her tap shoes as Geoffrey moves away from Andy, leaving her totally deflated ... and the others talk in busy little groups, Dorothy going to her handbag to take out a tissue to blow her nose. Sylvia moves towards Dorothy as

Mrs Fraser (*still reading*) Cause for celebration all round by the sound of it. Have you told him yet?
Mavis What? (*But, realizing*) I don't have to, thanks.
Mrs Fraser I see. False alarm was it?

Mavis (*with a flat smile*) Something like that. (*Generally*) You'll need the hats, please.

Sylvia Been busy this week, have you, Dorothy?

Dorothy Sorry?

Sylvia Been working hard, have we?

Dorothy I'm sorry, Sylvia, I don't——

Sylvia Understand—yes. Well I'll tell you: my Terry had one of your mates round this morning, one of your butter-wouldn't-melt bleeding inspectors. Making myself clear, am I?

Dorothy I'm sorry, Sylvia, I still don't——

Sylvia Understand—no. Someone's been snooping on him, Dorothy—and what fascinates me is where they got their information from.

Dorothy But I wouldn't.

Sylvia Well someone did, didn't they?

Mavis OK everyone. There's just one change I want to make and from then on we'll keep running it until it's really clean and tight—yes? Can I have the tape please, Lynne?

Lynne Sorry.

She takes the cassette from her Walkman as Mavis gets the cassette player from her bag

Mrs Fraser Do I take it that my presence is no longer required?

Mavis There isn't honestly much for you to do tonight, Glenda . . .

Lynne gives her the tape

Thanks Lynne . . . If you want to stay, it's really up to you.

Mrs Fraser I'm quite capable of occupying my time elsewhere, thank you.

Mavis Fine.

Mrs Fraser Just as long as I know. (*She collects up her things*)

Andy now looks totally withdrawn. Dorothy is still shaken

Mavis (*moving to Andy*) You'll be all right, will you, Andy?

Andy Oh—yes—(*she fingers the bandage*)—it's just a slight sprain.

Mrs Fraser is ready to leave

Mavis Good-night Glenda—thank you.

Vera Are you going, Mrs Fraser?

Mrs Fraser makes a bristling exit

Isn't she staying then?

Mavis (*clapping her hands*) OK—so the first thing I want to say is that you're all still looking at the floor.

Maxine All of us.

Mavis Most of you—anywhere but out front—they want to see your face not your roots—and *smile*—if you don't enjoy it, they won't enjoy it, yes?

Dorothy The three T's.

Sylvia Clever old Dorothy.

Andy (*hand up*) You said you wanted to change something.

Dorothy I didn't, Sylvia, honestly.

Mavis It's only one step, don't panic. Right, we'll have a look at that first. It's just before the last Fred Astaire—I want to add hats—(*she takes one of their hats*)—may I? Like this . . . (*She goes through the movement with the hat, chanting the step*) . . . OK? Try it . . .

She returns the hat and repeats the step . . . and they go through it . . . and Andy gets it wrong and drops her hat

OK?

Vera Mavis.

Mavis Yes Vera.

Vera What happens if someone drops their hat?

Mavis Good point—if you drop your hat—leave it—whatever you do, don't try and pick it up—just leave it, OK?

Vera Yes, I thought so.

Andy What you mean is, if *I* drop my hat.

Mavis No, if anyone——

Andy You mean me. That's what you meant, isn't it, Vera?

Maxine Don't be so touchy all the time.

Andy I didn't ask for your opinion, thank you.

Rose Come on, come on.

Mavis We've got plenty of time to work on it, I promise you.

Lynne Yes, don't worry, Andy.

Mavis OK? So it's . . . (*She begins to go through the step again, but*)

Andy I'm sorry but I really want to have this thing out.

Mavis All right Andy—what's the problem?

Andy I know exactly what you're thinking. All of you.

Maxine Oh gawd.

Andy You don't think I should be in it, you think I'm letting you down.

General ad-libbing . . . "Don't be silly, Andy . . ." "Why should anyone think . . ." etc. Mavis, knowing she's got trouble, reaches for a cigarette as

Lynne You're very good, Andy.

Andy *Please.*

Dorothy You are, you're very good.

Andy I am not good. I am not—good.

Mavis Andy . . .

Andy I don't know why I'm here, I don't know why I come, I can't do it, I can't *do* it. (*She wretchedly twists the hat in her hands*)

Vera But that's what we all admire about you, Andy . . .

Mavis Vera . . .

Vera The way you try so hard.

Sylvia Triffic.

Mavis Leave this to me, will you, Vera?

Vera Well I'm only trying to be helpful.

Andy I don't want you to be helpful . . . I'm sick and tired of you being helpful, you stupid stupid woman!

Mavis (*gently*) All right, Andy, all right.

Vera I really don't think there's any——
Andy You were just the same at the last class you went to . . . you didn't
leave because you didn't like the teacher you left because they asked you
to leave—because they couldn't stand your bloody interfering all the time
. . . well I'm sick of you, I'm sick of this, I'm sick of all of it. (*Close to tears,
she drops her hat—which only serves to increase her misery as she looks
down at it*) Oh—fuck.

She hurries into the changing room. Mavis goes in after her

A moment

Vera That isn't true actually: I left because I wanted to leave . . .
Rose Yes, all right all right Vera.
Maxine What we have here . . . is the makings of a real under the pier show.
Vera I can't help it if certain people . . .
Sylvia D'you mind if I ask you something, Vera: why don't you give it a rest
every now and again?

Rose nudges Sylvia, miming "Leave her" as

Maxine Listen—it was bound to happen—it's been on the cards for weeks.
Rose She's a very nervous woman.
Lynne Perhaps she's got cause to be.
Dorothy She swore.
Maxine She'll be all right once she's had her little cry.
Lynne You think so, do you?
Maxine I certainly hope so, darling.
Vera I suppose you think I should apologize.
Sylvia (*a warning finger*) Don't you dare.

Vera sits in front of the stage, as

Maxine (*placating*) OK—so what are we going to do?
Lynne There's nothing we can do, is there?
Maxine I don't mean her.
Lynne No, you wouldn't.
Maxine What does that mean?
Lynne Oh . . . nothing. (*She sits*)
Maxine Oh I get it, it's open the box time—OK—so does anyone else want
to say something? We've got nothing else to do, why not? Rose? Dorothy?
Sylvia She's said enough.
Dorothy I didn't—honestly.
Sylvia Well someone did, didn't they, Dorothy?
Rose What's all that about?
Sylvia I said—mind your own.
Rose Don't talk to me like that.
Dorothy She's accusing me of things I haven't done . . . (*a general plea*) . . . I
wouldn't do a thing like that, why would I do a thing like that?
Maxine Jesus Christ not another one.
Lynne (*moving closer to Dorothy*) What's happened?

Dorothy shakes her head, but

Sylvia They're turning my Terry over, that's what's happened.
Rose Who's they?
Sylvia (*pointing to Dorothy*) Her lot.
Dorothy I'm not even in the same department—anyway, I just wouldn't.
Sylvia Wouldn't—no.
Maxine Come on girls—we're here to enjoy ourselves.
Sylvia I am enjoying myself.
Rose Geoffrey—come the man, come the moment.
Geoffrey Sorry?
Rose Exert the masculine authority.
Geoffrey Yes, well I . . . (*he takes up Andy's fallen hat*) . . . I really don't see
    why . . . she'll obviously . . . I mean, after all, as Maxine said . . .
Sylvia (*flatly*) Let's hear it for the voice of authority.
Geoffrey (*rising slightly*) I really don't think we should involve ourselves
Maxine Of course you don't—but then you don't think it's right to get
    involved in anything, do you Geoffrey?
Geoffrey Not if it's none of my business—no.
Maxine I get a lot of people like you in my shop—they look but they never
    buy.
Geoffrey I find that very surprising—with you behind the till.
Maxine (*pointing*) Sharp.
Geoffrey Listening to you every week, I've had a good teacher.
Maxine And I thought you enjoyed being with the girls.
Geoffrey You know nothing about me—nothing.
Maxine (*spreading her hands*) So educate me—what is there to know?
Rose (*stepping in, brightly*) Does anyone want to have a go at *me*?
Sylvia Hello—big Ada's joined the fray.
Rose No-one? No-one want to have a go at the token spade?
Sylvia We only discuss your many and colourful faults behind your back.
Rose (*pseudo-shock*) No.
Sylvia Satisfied?
Rose Well don't say I didn't offer.
Maxine Sit down, Rose—your roots are showing.
Sylvia Better still—sing us a song.

Rose begins to hum softly, gently, and, after a moment:

Geoffrey Don't you think someone ought to find out what's happening?
Dorothy I'll go, shall I?
Sylvia Yeah, go on Dorothy—find out what's happening. (*Her tone implies
that maybe she was wrong in attacking Dorothy*)

Dorothy (*standing up*) I didn't, Sylvia.

Sylvia reaches up to take Dorothy's hand

Sylvia I believe you, thousands wouldn't—go on, go and find out what's
    happening.

A moment, and Dorothy goes into the changing room

Vera has been occupying herself by pointedly going through her handbag

Rose How many you got coming then, Vera?
Vera Pardon? Oh ... sorry—just my husband and daughter actually.
Rose That's nice.
Vera (*brightening*) Yes, they're looking forward to it. Are yours coming?
Rose Just my daughter. My husband say he prefer to wait for the video.

Rose moves to sit next to Vera as

Sylvia Coming for a drink after, Geoffrey?
Geoffrey (*smiling slightly*) Oh yes?
Sylvia Come on, come for a drink.

Dorothy comes out of the changing room

Dorothy They're just coming.
Maxine She's all right, is she?
Dorothy I think she's embarrassed more than anything. Mavis is being really nice to her.
Maxine Yeah, well ... we'll have to make sure we all are, won't we, Lynne?

Lynne looks at her and nods slightly. Vera is showing Rose a photograph album she has taken from her bag

Vera Yes she is like me, isn't she? (*She smiles at the photo*) She isn't Lionel's daughter, he adopted her. I was married before you see. I was very young and it didn't last. I met Lionel in Birmingham, he was up for the heavy vehicles exhibition and I was working in this club. I didn't want to but I had baby to support ... it was very respectable ... but some of the women ... you know. He was such a gentleman, Lionel. He still is. Well, you can see.

Lynne crosses to Maxine and sits next to her

Lynne (*quietly, to Maxine*) Andy was in out-patients yesterday. I didn't see her myself—I saw her name on the file when it came down from X-ray and later on I heard them talking about her. They don't think she just sprained her wrist—she's been there before apparently. They think it's her husband. They think she gets beaten up.
Maxine Oh Christ.
Rose Sylvie ... have you seen Lionel?

Vera takes the album for the others to see

Vera He's a lot older than me of course—I was only nineteen actually but we had an amazing time, amazing. It was him who taught me all about dress and everything—well, he has a lot of entertaining to do, a lot of people from Italy and places and they know about these things, don't they? And he sent me to cookery classes and oh, everything really. He said, "I don't want to be ashamed of you, do I?" He says some terrible things sometimes but it's only his sense of humour—you know—very dry. We went everywhere together, he looked after me so well and he was a wonderful lover, wonderful. I'd only been with my husband before and he was—well, he wasn't very delicate. But Lionel was wonderful. Of course, he's nearly sixty now, so it's not so . . . you know. And he thinks the world of Louise. She's seventeen now, Lionel says she's exactly like I was when he first met me. They go everywhere together, theatres, concerts, everywhere. I don't mind, I've got plenty to do and I enjoy making a nice home for them and anyway, they talk about things I don't really understand. She wants to work abroad but Lionel isn't sure, he really worries about her. Well, she's only a child really, isn't she?

Suddenly Mrs Fraser makes a glowering entrance. She surveys them

Mrs Fraser I see: having a little rest, are we? (*She crosses to the piano in a way that suggests that something a little stronger than carrot juice has passed her lips*)
Lynne We thought you'd gone home, Mrs Fraser.
Mrs Fraser (*with massive dignity*) Did you really?
Dorothy Has anything happened?
Sylvia She's been at the carrot juice.
Mrs Fraser I have come back to make one thing quite clear. Which is . . . that what I do here—as a favour to the vicar I might add—is a very small part of a very considerable repertoire. (*With no more ado, she launches into a spirited rendition of Chopin's "Revolutionary"*)

Dorothy takes the opportunity of doing some ballet steps to this music . . . and Vera takes the opportunity of showing those who haven't seen it her photograph album . . .

The Lights fade to Black-out and at the same time the sound of magnified piano-playing of the "Revolutionary" comes up, which continues as the curtains close. And then the piano-playing fades as we fade up to half-light on the closed Curtains for the next scene

SCENE 5

The night of the dress rehearsal. Off-stage, the sound of someone using a hammer. The Curtains are still closed

After a moment, Mavis pushes her way through the centre of the Curtains, holding a hand microphone and shading her eyes as she looks up towards the back of the auditorium

Mavis Mavis Turner, Item Number Six.

No response

Hello? Hello?

[*As she says this, a very large sugar plum fairy in tutu and clutching one eye wanders on from the wings*

Fairy Hello ... I've lost my contact lens.

She goes behind Mavis and through the Curtains

Mavis watches her, bewildered, for a moment, and then turns back to call up]

Mavis What's happening to the curtain?

No reply

Can you hear me or what?

Man's voice (*on microphone distort*) Yes, all right darling, I can hear you.

The banging continues as

Mavis So what's happening?

Man's voice Nigel's having a spot of trouble.

Mavis Nigel isn't the only one—so how long are you going to be?

Man's voice We've had nine sugar plum fairies, three country and western and A Night In Old Vienna, we're doing our best.

The Curtains open. The stage is in darkness

Mavis Can I have a working light please?

The working light comes up. The stage is draped in blue curtains on all three sides and is bare apart from a white cupid on a plinth, left there from the last rehearsal [*... and two sugar plum fairies on their hands and knees, backs towards us, searching for the missing contact lens*

Fairy I found it!

She triumphantly shows the lens to Mavis and the two fairies go off through the wings

Mavis She's found it] ... can we try the spot, please?

A spot beams down, R *... on Mrs Fraser who stands scowling beneath her hat, bag over her arm*

Mavis moves towards her

(*Still into the microphone*) OK ... so he starts here and I want the spot to widen and—stop the bloody banging!

The banging stops

Thank you. I want the——

Two or three short sharp bangs of the hammer

Always a comedian. I want the spot to——

Man's voice You want a follow spot—yes, all right darling, I heard you.

Mavis Can we try it please?

Man's voice Whenever you're ready.

Mavis Just run through it for me, will you, Glenda?

She moves Mrs Fraser to C, *the spot going with her, and stands back as Mrs Fraser scowls up into the spotlight and throws out an arm for each number as she counts*

Mrs Fraser One ... two ... three ... four ... five——
Man's voice Et cetera et cetera—OK—got you.
Mrs Fraser (*persisting through this*) —six ... seven.
Mavis Thank you, Glenda.
Mrs Fraser Oh that's it, is it?
Mavis That's it—thank you—you wouldn't like to rustle up some tea or something, would you?

Mrs Fraser exits, R, *through the wings*

The spots goes out

So we start with the——
Man's voice You want the cyc and boomer to start, in with the spot, bring up the front of house and kill the spot. Next?
Mavis (*with a flat smile*) Can we have the curtain down, please?
Man's voice Curtain please, Nigel.
Mavis And another notch up on the sound—yes?
Man's voice For you darling, the lot.
Mavis And—er ... (*She indicates the cupid*)
Man's voice (*shouting*) And strike that cupid!

As the Curtain comes down, Nigel enters through the wings, L, *grabs the cupid and exits,* R, *with it, as*

Nigel It's not my job ... I'm fed up with doing other peoples' work, I am, I'm fed up.

He exits R

By now the Curtains are closed and Mavis is outside them, to one side, holding the microphone

Mavis OK everyone—opening positions please.

We can hear the dancers hurrying on in their tap shoes and suddenly the opening bars of the number strike up and panic breaks out behind the Curtain

Not yet, not yet!

The music stops

Man's voice Sorry ladies, our mistake—whenever you're ready.
Mavis Say when you're ready, Lynne.
Some more scuffling from behind the Curtains and then a plaintive

Lynne Ready.
Mavis Ready when you are.
Man's voice Five seconds.

Sylvia Oh my gawd!

A brief moment . . . and then the music strikes up . . . "Stepping Out" . . . and the Curtains rise . . . and we are into our routine. The dancers, in their boaters and striped blazers, go through their number with Mavis offering encouragement and instruction through the microphone . . .

In the part where they each do their solo bit with Geoffrey . . . Dorothy is too enthusiastic and spins off into the curtains . . . Maxine takes the opportunity to do a bit on her own, C facing out front . . . and they get to the end and stop in good and uniform time. Mavis comes on to congratulate them . . . and they are milling around, pleased and excited as

Mavis That was really good, everyone, well done! (*To the unseen Man*) We'll go again whenever you're ready, please. (*To the class again*) Just a few points—Lynne, you're still late on the pickup . . . Rose, you've stopped hiding but you're leaning . . . Dorothy, watch the arms . . . Andy—well done!

As she is speaking and they are reacting with pleasure, the Curtain comes down

Just as Mrs Fraser is entering from the wings, R . . . carrying a trayload of plastic cups of tea . . . so that she finds herself stuck, outside the Curtain . . . and a spot hits her as she moves C and tries and fails to get through the Curtain. Realizing, as though for the first time, that she is being watched by the audience . . . she jerks her head back haughtily and exits with the tray into the wings, R

As she does, the spot goes out and there is a roll of drums

2nd Man's voice Ladies and gentlemen! Due to an unprecedented public response to their appearance here last year . . . we are proud to present the return of the Mavis Turner Tappers!

And the musical introduction strikes up as a lime wanders round the Curtain like a bouncing ball and the Curtains open and the stage lights come up and there is now a silver slash over the blue curtains

The class go into their final choreographed tap routine . . . with all the class and Mavis taking part in top hats, tails and with telescopic canes . . . and Mrs Frazer joining in, in black gown and tiara . . . and the routine comes to an end with the company forming into a group and——

the CURTAIN *falls*

As a Curtain call . . . the Curtain slowly rises, showing a line of tapping feet . . . a nod towards "42nd Street" . . .

FURNITURE AND PROPERTY LIST

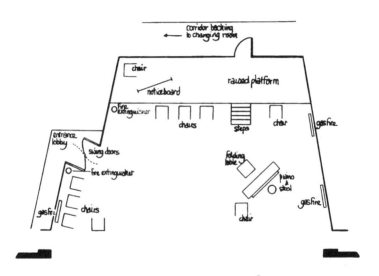

ACT I

SCENE 1

On stage: Upright chairs. *On them:* **Dorothy**'s handbag; **Maxine**'s coat and bag
 containing leotards in plastic packs, tap shoes, **Andy**'s coat and bag
 containing tap shoes, purse and money
3 gas-fires
2 fire extinguishers
Notice-board. *On it:* notices, posters, pins etc.
Curtains at sides of raised stage area
Upright piano and stool. *On piano:* music, magazine and apple for **Mrs
 Fraser**. *Next to it:* **Mrs Fraser**'s bag
Folding table. *On it:* register, cashbox, cigarettes and lighter for **Mavis**,
 ashtray, carton of fruit juice. *Near it:* **Mavis'** canvas bag containing tap
 shoes, car keys

Off stage: Carrier bag, leotard in plastic pack **(Middle-aged Woman)**
Crash helmet **(Young Woman)**
Briefcase containing practice clothes, tap boots **(Geoffrey)**
Keys **(Geoffrey)**
Handbag **(Dorothy)**
Bag with tap shoes **(Vera)**

Personal: **Andy:** glasses *(required throughout)*
Maxine: large rings on fingers *(required throughout)*
Rose: wig, crucifix, lots of rings
Sylvia: chewing gum
Vera: handkerchief

SCENE 2

Strike: All bags and coats except **Geoffrey**'s
Register, cashbox

Set: Tidy and straighten chairs
Sandwich in clingfilm for **Geoffrey**
Geoffrey's shoes under chair
Wastebin by piano

Off stage: Bag containing flask of coffee, sugar, spoon, Harrods bag **(Vera)**
Bag containing tap shoes **(Andy)**
Bag containing new tap shoes, money for Scene 3 **(Sylvia)**
Bag containing tap shoes **(Rose)**
Bag with tap shoes, 2 shirts in plastic packs, cigarettes, lighter, brush for Scene 3 **(Maxine)**
Yellow safety harness, bike basket with handbag, lamp, pump, dance gear **(Dorothy)**
Bag **(Andy)**
Handbag **(Dorothy)**
Wastebin, 2 ashtrays **(Vera)**
Canvas bag containing tap shoes; cigarettes, lighter, register, cashbox for Scene 3; music case **(Mavis)**
Bag containing magazine for Scene 3 **(Mrs Fraser)**

Personal: **Geoffrey:** lighter, key
Sylvia: chewing gum
Rose: wig, crucifix, rings

SCENE 3

Set: 2 empty orange juice cartons, banana skin on piano
Magazine by piano for **Mrs Fraser**
Cigarettes, lighter for **Mavis**, register, cashbox on folding table
Petition and pen near **Andy**'s bag
Sock over back of chair
2 T-shirts in plastic packs by **Maxine**'s bag
Gold belt over chair

Off stage: Bag **(Rose)**
Bag with mirror, comb **(Vera)**
Bike basket with handbag, lamp etc. **(Dorothy)**
Bag **(Lynne)**

Personal: **Sylvia:** chewing gum
          Rose: wig, crucifix, rings

SCENE 4

Set: Tidy and straighten chairs
          Mavis' bag, cigarettes, lighter, coat etc. by folding table
          Exercise book on floor
          Register, cashbox on folding table

Off stage: Bag containing dance gear **(Lynne)**
          Bag containing money, dance gear **(Maxine)**
          Yellow safety harness **(Dorothy)**
          Bicycle with basket containing dance gear, handbag **(Dorothy)**
          Bag, music case, magazine **(Mrs Fraser)**
          Briefcase containing dance gear, money **(Geoffrey)**
          Bag containing dance gear, money **(Rose)**
          Bag containing dance gear **(Sylvia)**
          Bag containing dance gear, money **(Vera)**
          Handbag containing money **(Dorothy)**
          Bag containing dance gear, money **(Andy)**

Personal: **Rose:** wig, crucifix, rings
          Sylvia: chewing gum

ACT II

SCENE 1

Strike: Bike etc.

Personal: **Sylvia:** chewing gum
          Rose: rings, crucifix

SCENE 2

Set: Canes for whole class
          Mavis' exercise book on floor
          Key on table
          Maxine's lighter on floor under chair

Off stage: Bag **(Rose)**
          Rubber gloves, aerosol spray **(Vera)**
          Bike basket with handbag, lamp etc. **(Dorothy)**
          Bag **(Andy)**
          Bag **(Lynne)**
          Bandage on finger **(Geoffery)**
          Bag **(Vera)**

SCENE 3

Strike: **Maxine's** cane
          Sylvia's cane

Set: Tidy and straighten chairs
         Andy's bag and cane
         Sylvia's bag and cane with painted bottom
         Lynne's bag and cane
         Geoffrey's briefcase and cane on stage behind notice-board
         Vera's cane
         Electric fan (practical), plug, penknife for **Geoffrey**
         Dorothy's handbag, cane, box of tissues
         Mavis' bag, cigarettes, lighter, cane, exercise book, register, cashbox on
             folding table
         Mrs Fraser's bag, magazine, music case by piano

Off stage: Bag containing tap shoes, cane, large box with 6 assorted hats, tied with
             string **(Maxine)**
             Cigarettes, lighter **(Mavis)**

SCENE 4

Strike: All canes
           Fan
           Box of tissues
           Dorothy's handbag

Set: Tidy and straighten chairs
           Striped blazers for whole class
           Fishnet stockings in packets for **Maxine**
           Box of pins for **Vera**
           Straw boaters for whole class
           Poster near notice-board for **Mavis**
           Dyed black tap shoes and diary in **Andy**'s bag
           Pen and paper near piano
           Personal stereo with tape for **Lynne**
           Cassette player in **Mavis**' bag
           Vera's bag containing photograph album by stage

Off stage: Bike basket with dance gear etc., handbag **(Dorothy)**
             Handbag containing tissues **(Dorothy)**
             Bag, music case **(Mrs Fraser)**

Personal: **Andy:** bandage round hand and wrist
             Geoffrey: sheet of paper in pocket

SCENE 5

Strike: All props and furniture

Set: Drapes on 3 sides
           White cupid on plinth

Off stage: Hand microphone (practical) **(Mavis)**
             Handbag **(Mrs Fraser)**
             Trayload of plastic cups of tea **(Mrs Fraser)**
             During Black-out on page 72: set silver slash over drapes
             Telescopic canes **(Company)**

LIGHTING PLOT

Practical fittings required: 3 gas fires, several pendants, lights in entrance lobby and changing room

Interior. A church hall, another hall

ACT I, SCENE 1.   Evening

To open: General interior lighting—all practicals on

Cue 1	**Geoffrey** switches off gas fires *Cut fire effects*	(Page 7)
Cue 2	Class finish "Tea For Two" routine *Quick Black-out*	(Page 10)

ACT I, SCENE 2.   Evening

To open: General interior lighting—pendants on, lights in entrance lobby and changing room on

Cue 3	**Geoffrey** lights gas fires *Bring up fire effects as he lights each one*	(Page 12)
Cue 4	Class dance to "I Got Rhythm" *Fast change to blue. When ready up to full*	(Page 19)

ACT I, SCENE 3.   Evening

Cue 5	**Mrs Fraser** reaches up to turn off light *Black-out*	(Page 26)

ACT I, SCENE 4.   Evening

To open: General interior lighting—all practicals on

Cue 6	Class stop dancing, holding arms outstretched pose *Black-out*	(Page 33)

ACT II, SCENE 1.   Evening

To open: General interior lighting—all practicals on

Cue 7	Class attempt new steps, getting it hopelessly wrong *Black-out*	(Page 39)

ACT II, SCENE 2.   Evening

To open: General interior lighting—all practicals on except fires

Cue 8   **Andy** bangs piano keys violently   (Page 46)
             Black-out

ACT II, SCENE 3.   Evening

To open: General interior lighting—all practicals on except fires

Cue 9   Class dance like lifeless puppets   (Page 56)
             Black-out

ACT II, SCENE 4.   Evening

To open: General interior lighting—all practicals on except fires

Cue 10   **Mrs Fraser** plays Chopin's "Revolutionary" on piano   (Page 66)
             Fade to Black-out

ACT II, SCENE 5.   Evening

To open: Half-light on closed curtains

Cue 11   **Mavis:** "Can I have a working light, please?"   (Page 67)
             Bring up working light

Cue 12   **Mavis:** "... try the spot, please?"   (Page 67)
             Snap on spot, R, *on* **Mrs Fraser**

Cue 13   **Mavis** moves **Mrs Fraser** C   (Page 68)
             Follow **Mrs Fraser** *with spot*

Cue 14   **Mrs Fraser** exits R   (Page 68)
             Cut spot

Cue 15   **Sylvia:** "Oh my gawd!"   (Page 69)
             Bring up general lighting on stage

Cue 16   Introduction to "Stepping Out" begins (*2nd time*)   (Page 69)
             Spot wandering over curtains like bouncing ball

Cue 17   Curtains open   (Page 69)
             Bring up bright general lighting on stage

EFFECTS PLOT

ACT I

Cue 1   Black-out   (Page 10)
                  Music: orchestrated version of "Happy Feet" underscored with
                  heavy tap dancing

Cue 2   When ready for Scene 2   (Page 11)
                  Cut music

Cue 3   Black-out   (Page 26)
                  Music: "Happy Feet"

Cue 4   When ready for Scene 4   (Page 26)
                  Cut music

Cue 5   Black-out   (Page 33)
                  Music: orchestrated version of "Let's Face The Music And
                  Dance"

ACT II

Cue 6   Black-out   (Page 39)
                  Music: "Happy Feet"

Cue 7   When ready for Scene 2   (Page 39)
                  Cut music

Cue 8   **Andy** plays same note on piano   (Page 46)
                  Car horn, off

Cue 9   Black-out   (Page 46)
                  Music: "Happy Feet"

Cue 10   When ready for Scene 3   (Page 46)
                  Cut music

Cue 11   **Vera** switches on fan   (Page 47)
                  Fan noise

Cue 12   **Vera** switches off fan   (Page 49)
                  Cut fan noise

Cue 13   Black-out   (Page 56)
                  Music: "Happy Feet"

Cue 14   When ready for Scene 4   (Page 56)
                  Cut music

Cue 15   Black-out   (Page 66)
                  Music: magnified piano-playing of Chopin's "Revolutionary"

DANCE NOTES

The steps referred to here are the one used in the West End production of the play. They are given here as suggestions for the type of dances to be used, but can be altered or amended as desired

ACT I

WARM-UP (Page 7) to the music of "The Entertainer"

1. Four knee bends, using arms also
2. Three toe taps using right toe first: front, side, back diag., together. Repeat to left
3. Four shuffle downs using right foot first: R, L, R, L
4. Eight pick-ups going back. Arms outstretched to front, palms front
5. Tap springs starting with R foot. 1, 2, 3 clap. L foot. 1, 2, 3, clap, then eight tap springs
6. Tap step heel starting R foot and going R diagonal three times, shuffle ball, change direction. Repeat to L. Use arms in opposition

Cue: **Mavis:** "Evening Rose, nice of you to join us."
Repeat whole sequence from shuffle downs

ROUTINE (Page 9) to the music of "Tea for Two"

Cue: **Mavis:** "Basically it's three buffalos to the right followed by a cramp roll, then to the left. Four scoots R, L, R, L and six tap springs in a circle and tap step, stamp stamp."
1. Three buffalos, one cramp roll to R. Repeat to L
2. Four scoots R diag and back, L diag and back, R diag and back, L diag and back
3. Six tap springs circle R
4. Tap step, stamp stamp (facing front)

ROUTINE (Page 19) to the music of "I Got Rhythm"

Cue: **Mavis:** "So it's one cramp roll, slap thigh, R, L, click fingers R, L. Repeat. Scissors to R and then L times three. Pick up, heel, step."
1. One cramp roll (R foot brush R toe, L toe, R heel, L heel)
2. R hand slap R thigh, L hand slap L thigh. Click fingers R and L
3. Repeat from 1
4. Scissors (double—to R. (step R cross L front, step R cross L behind, step R cross L front, step R extend L) Repeat to L. (Arms in opposition on extended foot)
5. Flap R, clap R diag. Flap L, clap L diag. Flap R clap R diag, shuffle, ball change, L diag.

6. Pick up heel step backwards to USL
   TABS DOWN, END OF SCENE 2

ROUTINE (Page 19) to music of "I Got Rhythm". (middle, eight, stop chorus)

TABS UP
 1. Stamp R, stamp L. Shuffle ball change step twice. R diag.
 2. Going to L in circle. Brush hop, brush hop (forward and back). NB. Brush with
    DS (R) foot first time. Tap step, ball change four times
 3. Facing front, weight on to R heel then L heel flick back R flick back L, stamp R
    stamp L, pick up R, pick up L. Arms front outstretched
 4. To R tap spring, clap, tap spring, clap, three tap springs, clap, clap
 5. Train step LRL, RLR, LRL, RLR, stamp, stamp R foot (no weight on last
    stamp)
 6. Repeat from 4 to the left
 7. Seven tap springs forward, stamp
    NB. From 4, music increases speed to end
    Mavis: "Well done everyone, that was really good, yes?"

ROUTINE (Page 33) to the music "Let's Face the Music and Dance"

Cue: **Mavis:** "Whenever you're ready Glenda ... and ... five, six, seven, eight ..."
 1. Four shuffle hop steps
 2. Four pick ups going back
 3. Four tap springs
 4. Jump on to R shuffle L, shuffle R, shuffle L
 5. Heel R, heel L, back R, back L (flat feet)
 6. Three paddles back (heel brush forward, toe brush back, toe heel) stamp
 7. Four trenchs
 8. Brush out heel, brush back, heel, tap, stop, ball change, repeat to L
 9. Stamp R in, out, in, out
10. Coupe under pull back to UL diagonal. Ball change pull back to UR diagonal
    Fast shuffles as in 2nd part of 4 to finish
    NB. Left foot finished forward after step shuffle (14) R arm out whether ball
    change or not and to start that section step on L and shuffle with R

FINALE—"STEPPING OUT" (Concert version) (Page 69)

	Andy	Sylvia	Rose
Lynne	Vera	Maxine	Dorothy
		Geoff	
		(DSC)	

All facing US. L hand on small of back. R hand touching hat
Four counts for nothing
1st count of next bar. Back line turn holding hat high in R hand and L arm in second
1st count of next bar middle line turn holding hat in R hand and left arm in low
    second
3rd count Geoffery turns as back line
All sway R and L, draw feet together with both arms and hat held above head high
    (these last two movements are simultaneous)
Bring hat down on to head on 4th count

Dance to "Stepping Out"

1st Chorus
 1. Three toe taps to R diag (Fred—Ast—aire) holding hat in both hands at chest level
 2. Box step (L foot over R) bring hat on to head on last step of box
 3. Drop arms to side. Three tap springs R, L, R. Tap hat with R hand. L hand on hip
 4. Drop arms to side on shuffle hop step L then R
 5. Four shuffle ball changes with L foot, circling to R, lifting hat high in R hand
 6. Six tap springs into line DS starting on L foot. At the same time drawing arms above head and bringing hat down on last count

Lynne   Andy   Vera   Geoff   Sylvia   Maxine   Rose   Dorothy

2nd Chorus
 1. Three toe taps to R diag (Fred—Ast—aire). Hats on chest
 2. Two train steps L, R, L and R, L, R. Stamp R, stamp L. Pick up R and L, fast pick up R and ball change, leaving L foot forward. At the same time as ball change place hats on head
 3. Cramp roll starting on R foot. Two stamps R and L
 4. Eight pick up steps travelling backwards to diag SL all holding little fingers, apart from Geoff who travels to USC
 5. Shuffle hop step R over L. Tap step, ball change, starting on L. Shuffle hop step R over L. Stamp L

Middle 8—Waltz time

 1. As everyone marks time with shuffle step R and L Lynne waltzes across Geoffrey, turning (for two waltz counts) into position DSR, picks up marking. Others follow with the same. Two counts each. (See diagram)

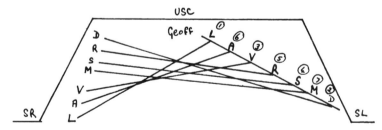

Last Chorus
 1. Travelling diagonally downstage to original line-up. Four step togethers, starting on L. Hats up and down. On last count hat on head
 2. Tap step, ball change three times starting on L. Stamp R
 3. Scuff R. Heel L. Pick up R and L. Repeat again on R. Arms opening to 2nd on scuff
 4. Two paddles R and L (stamp R, pick up toe, heel) Arms by side
 5. Stamp in out, in out R touching brims of hat with R hand

6. Step forward R, tilting hat forward. Pivot on L to face US. Step on R again, tilting hat. Pivot to face front. Weight on L
7. Fred—Ast—aire holding brim of hat R hand
8. Step together to L twice, turning knees out, lifting shoulders (as puppet)
9. Clap
10. Six tap springs starting on R. Finish stepping forward into R foot, holding hat out front

FINALE CHOREOGRAPHY by Tudor Davies

Cue: **2nd Man's Voice:** "... the return of Mavis Turner Tappers!" (Page 69)

      1st Dancer—Mavis
      2nd Dancer—Sylvia
      3rd Dancer—Maxine
      4th Dancer—Andy
      5th Dancer—Vera
      6th Dancer—Lynne
      7th Dancer—Dorothy
      8th Dancer—Rose

1. 1st Chorus of "Top Hat, White Tie and Tails"

Enter USR 1st Dancer, with R hand on hat, L hand on small of back, facing front but travelling laterally:
Tap step, heel L. Repeat R across L. Stamp L.
Pick up step R. Rep. L.
Shuffle hop step R over L, catching L toe behind R heel.
Drop R heel

2nd Dancer enters as 1st. Repeat above.
3rd Dancer enters as 1 and 2. Repeat above. 3 times in all.
All end on a lunge L, in profile facing SL. L heel raised. Hands as above.

Fig. 1

        3   2   1
          DS

Dancers 4, 5 and 6 enter DSR. Step on to R, brush L. Hop R. Step L (clog-step). 8 times R to L, ending in profile as above. (N.B. Arms swing in opposition on clog-step with elbows bent.)

Fig. 2

         3   2   1
     6   5   4
          DS

2. 2nd Chorus

On last beat of 1st Chorus US line turns to face front. Both hands behind back.
Pick up step R, Repeat L. Pick up step ball change R. Repeat L.
On last beat of last phase DS line turns and joins in repeat of Pick Up, etc.

All take 8 clog-steps, starting R travelling L to get into following positions:

Fig. 3

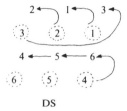

DS

All take 4 clog-steps facing front. DS line travelling US. US line travelling DS to end:

Fig. 4

```
        4       5       6
            2       1       3
                   DS
```

(N.B. On last 4 clog-steps, arms swing in front with elbows bent, palms front, fingers spread. Body bent slightly forward)
All brush R leg out and back across L. Place R on ball. At the same time L hand mimes pulling R cuff down. Swing shoulders. Look sharply over R shoulder. All stay in position as:

3. Middle Eight

Dancers 7 and 8 enter CSR, facing US. R hand to hat. L hand on small of back. Palms facing. Travelling laterally.
4 slow walks. Starting L crossing R over L.
4 quick walks round to face front to end:

Fig. 5

```
        4       5       6
            8       7
        2       1       3
                DS
```

All sway R-L-R. Palms out front (window-cleaning).
Drop on to R, both knees bent. L heel raised. Head L.
Ball change L behind R. Step L.
Swivel to face R. R heel raised. Peel L leg through in front of R. At the same time drop L hand to side, R hand to hat.
Drop L heel, out, in, out. Draw both legs together to face US. L hand on small of back. Palms out.
Clips heels twice.
Walk US R and L. Turn to R. Walk DS, R and L, ending with L knee bent. Heel raised.
1st Dancer does 4 quick stamps R.

4. 3rd Chorus

All swing R arm to side of hat as R knee bends, heel raised (as though saluting)
4 double time steps to front, R L. Hands to chest, elbows bent.
On 5th time-step turn to L. Diagonal.
Do half of 6th time-step. Drop on to R. R arm low, L arm high.

Shuffle L. Ball change. Arms to chest.
Stamp R. Arms on diag.
Shuffle L. Ball change. Arms to chest.
2 stamps R. Arms in 5th. Palms out, on diag.

5. Middle Eight repeated as a Jazz Walz

On 1st count Dancers 1, 2 and 3 pas de bourrée under with L foot. Balance R. Arms following.
Balance L, relevé on to L, raising R leg, swing both arms in a circle clock-wise. R leg crosses L. Exit SL.
On 5th count Dancers 7 and 8 relevé L, raising R legs as above. Exit SL
Also on 5th count Dancers 4, 5 and 6 pas de bourrée etc as on 1st line. Exit SL.
(N.B. All exit on a small run. L arm raised to chest. R arm extended to side. Head L - mock balletic!)

Also on 1st count of this section Geoffrey enters DSR. Grande jeté entournant starting L to finish facing SR. 3 châiné turns to L. Balancé L as girls exit. Mrs Fraser enters DSR and drapes herself around the proscenium. Geoffrey takes 4 slow walks to Mrs Fraser taking her arm. 4 slow walks to C. Mrs Fraser continues to USC and curtseys, as Geoffrey walks around himself to end facing front C.
Single pirourette en dehors ending with a relevé R. L leg raised, arms in 3rd. Hat high in R hand. Drop to a deep lunge L facing SL. R arm forward.

6. 4th Chorus

On first count 8 dancers enter DSL in two lines

Fig. 6

                                    DS
8   6   5   4 travel across to SR and US to C. Spring cane in R hand
1   3   2   7 travel US to C and U turn. Spring cane in L hand

24 tap springs starting R to end:

Fig. 7

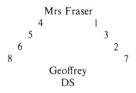

Mrs Fraser

SL line end facing L. Diag with L knee bent
SR line end facing R. Diag. with R knee bent
(N.B. Heads tilted over R shoulder on tap springs. R hand clenched to chest. Elbow at side. L hand clenched. Arm by side)

At the same time Geoffrey picks up tap springs, travels US and back to C.
On separate counts each corresponding pair releases cane. Starting DS 4 counts in all. Alternating knees on release.
On next two counts all point canes to C, across body. Draw cane sharply to underarm, again alternating knees.

At the same time as 1st cane release, Geoffrey travels DS -3 clog-steps starting R. 3 double wings with arms circulating. 5 drop shuffles starting R.
ALL take 2 clog-steps starting R to end in tableau. (N.B. Mrs Fraser sways *ad nauseum* until clog-steps)

Fig. 8

```
                        Mrs Fraser
                     Geoffrey          3
          5       4                 2      7
          8       6        1
                         DS                        (Various positions)
```

MADE AND PRINTED IN GREAT BRITAIN BY
LATIMER TREND & COMPANY LTD, PLYMOUTH
MADE IN ENGLAND